Got Religion?

Got Religion?

How Churches, Mosques, and Synagogues
Can Bring Young People Back

Naomi Schaefer Riley

TEMPLETON PRESS

Templeton Press
300 Conshohocken State Road, Suite 500
West Conshohocken, PA 19428
www.templetonpress.org

Designed and typeset by Gopa & Ted2, Inc.

ISBN-13: 978-1-59947-391-8

Library of Congress Cataloging-in-Publication Data on file.

Printed in the United States of America
14 15 16 17 18   10 9 8 7 6 5 4 3 2 1

Contents

Preface   vii

Introduction   1

1. Location, Location, Location: 17
   How the "Theology of Place" Is Plugging Young Adults
   Back into Their Communities and Their Churches

2. The All-American Mosque: 35
   How Shedding Immigrant Ways Can Reshape
   Islam in the United States

3. Joining the Service: 55
   How the Catholic Church Is Training a New
   Generation of Laypeople to Be Spiritual Leaders

4. What's NEXT?   73
   Channeling the Enthusiasm of Birthright Israel
   into a Permanent Jewish Commitment

5. A Ward of Their Own: 91
   How the Mormon Church Is Turning
   Twenty-Somethings into Community Leaders

6. When No One Needs Church Anymore,
   How Do You Make Them Want It?   107
   The Relevance of the Black Church in the
   Twenty-First Century

7. The End of Sheep Stealing: 123
   How Churches Can Collaborate
   to Bring Twenty-Somethings Back into the Fold

Conclusion   139

Notes   155

Index   157

Preface

A FEW YEARS AGO I was asked to join a committee at my synagogue that was tasked with figuring out how to make nursery school parents into more active synagogue members. Whatever else one could say about a drop-off in religious affiliation, these people—parents of young children—were supposed to be the ones we could count on to be active members. And yet week after week the vast majority of families did not come to synagogue. Maybe I was asked to be on the committee because I write about religion. Or maybe it's because I was part of the problem.

The committee organized focus groups and asked parents in their thirties and forties why they were willing to drop off their kids for preschool every morning but they weren't attending Shabbat services with them Saturdays or why they weren't volunteering more or why they weren't planning to sign the kids up for Hebrew school. The answers varied greatly. For some it was time; for others the service was not the sort they had grown up with; and for many, religious observance simply wasn't a priority.

But over and over, one line was repeated: "I'd come if I knew other people were coming."

Really? I began to grow frustrated (sometimes visibly so) when people offered this answer, wondering if I was talking to eighth-graders or grown-ups. *You'll come if other people come? If the cool kids come?* This seemed like such an absurd reason to stay home and at the same time something the leadership of the synagogue seemed to have very little ability to change.

There had to be some better way to think about getting, congregants involved. The frustration is even worse when it comes to singles and their religious practices. They aren't even setting foot in the door to use the preschool. So what would possess them to start thinking seriously about joining or participating in the life of a religious institution?

Like thousands of religious institutions around the country, mine has made a valiant effort to engage the unaffiliated and the disaffected. Though I am a little older than many of the people interviewed in this book and, more importantly, I am at a different stage of life (married with kids, not single), seeing why young adults don't bother with religious life is very easy for me. As the rabbi at Sixth and I, a popular synagogue in Washington, DC, told me, "We're not competing with other synagogues on Friday nights. Our competition is movies and plays and bars and restaurants and parties."

Nonetheless, seeing the appeal of the religious institutions young adults have chosen is easy. It's not only because the cool kids are attending. In the course of researching this book I found the ones they attach themselves to are not necessarily the biggest or the most flashy. They are not the wealthiest or the ones employing the latest technology. They are the ones that help young adults form the habits of believers.

The period we refer to as "emerging adulthood" is a kind of second adolescence—not because twenty-somethings are immature but because their lives are unstable in the same ways adolescent lives are. They're moving to new places, with new roommates. They're making new friends, dating different people, trying out new jobs, going back to school, making money, and going into debt. At this stage in life they don't give religious institutions a lot of consideration.

But our churches and synagogues and mosques actually have the opportunity to create some stability for them, to give them real responsibility in a community, to help them form those habits that could last a lifetime.

As the sun goes down on Friday night, Jews around the world

sing a medieval hymn—"Shalom Aleichem"—in which we wish peace upon the "ministering angels." Who are these angels? According to the Talmud, one good angel and one evil angel accompany a person home on Friday night from the synagogue. "When they arrive home, if they find a candle lit, the table set, and beds arranged nicely, the good angel says, 'May it be God's will that next Shabbat be the same,' and the evil angel is compelled to respond, 'Amen!' Otherwise, [if the home is not prepared in honor of Shabbat] the evil angel says, 'May it be God's will that next Shabbat be the same,' and the good angel is compelled to respond, 'Amen!'"

My own rabbi was recently discussing this passage, and he made an important observation—one more sociological than theological. The fact of the matter, he told a group of us gathered, is that "Next Shabbat *will* probably be the same." In other words, if you light the candles and say the blessing over the challah and the wine, if you have prepared a nice meal and set aside time for your family and friends this Friday night, you will probably do the same thing next week. If you don't, chances are you won't next week either.

That is both the happy and the sad truth about young adults and religion. The habits they form this week will affect next week, too. And all the years to come.

Introduction

IN A WIDELY discussed 2013 article in the *Atlantic* called "A Million First Dates," author Dan Slater wrote that "online romance is threatening monogamy." Men and women are simply not willing to offer the same amount of commitment because in the backs of their minds they are always aware of the other possibilities. Here's what one single man in his early thirties told Slater about the way Internet dating affected the way he viewed the end of a long-term relationship:

> I'm about 95 percent certain that if I'd met Rachel offline, and if I'd never done online dating, I would've married her. At that point in my life, I would've overlooked everything else and done whatever it took to make things work. Did online dating change my perception of permanence? No doubt. When I sensed the breakup coming, I was okay with it. It didn't seem like there was going to be much of a mourning period, where you stare at your wall thinking you're destined to be alone and all that. I was eager to see what else was out there.

"Eager to see what else is out there." That pretty much describes the modern world—especially the world through the eyes of twenty- and thirty-somethings. It has become cliché to point out that the array of choices we have today often leaves us more unhappy than a limited spectrum might have. *Have I bought the right shampoo or is there one of the thousands of others on the mar-*

ket I'd like better? Have I purchased the right house or will watching House Hunters *make me regret it? Have I chosen the right restaurant or will I want to be eating the meal that a friend on Facebook has just posted a picture of?* Between the explosion of products to meet every desire, the accessibility of such products online, and the changes in technology—both reality television and social media—we know something better is always out there, and we know that someone else has it.

How could such a world not affect our choice of romantic partners—and everything else?

Books on the millennial generation tend to go on at length about the so-called paradox of choice and the related phenomenon of decision fatigue. Twenty-somethings, they report, are paralyzed in the face of too many options and exhausted by having to pick among them.

And they also don't want to close anything off by actually making a decision. They worry that any choice they make will be too permanent. In their book *Twentysomething: Why Do Young Adults Seem Stuck?*, mother and daughter journalists Robin Marantz Henig and Samantha Henig cite a fascinating study demonstrating this tendency. In a computer game devised by MIT psychologists, young adult players are given a certain number of "clicks" that they can use to "open doors" or—once inside a room—get a small amount of money. After a few minutes of wandering, the players figure out which rooms have the most money. Theoretically they should simply keep clicking in those rooms. But sometimes, doors will start closing. Even players who know they will earn more from using their clicks inside a room will start to panic and click to keep the doors from closing.

In other words, even if the other possible directions for our lives are less valuable—even entirely implausible—we still don't want them to close.

The same month that Slater's article appeared, Barry Cooper penned a more theological description of this sense of generational panic in *Christianity Today*. Cooper wrote, "We are worshiping an idol. A false god. One of the Baals of our culture. His name is 'open options.'"

This false god "kills our relationships because He tells us it's better not to become too involved . . . He kills our giving because he tells us these are uncertain financial times and you never know when you need the money." Cooper concludes, "The god of open options is also a liar. He promises you that by keeping your options open, you can have everything and everyone. But in the end, you get nothing and no one."

These are the words of caution that many religious leaders would like to offer the millennial generation. Clergy, laypeople, teachers, parents, and grandparents are worried about this thing called "emerging adulthood," in which people seem to put off all the traditional markers of growing up—leaving home, becoming financially independent, getting married—in favor of this permanent merry-go-round of choices. This new phase of adulthood is diminishing the involvement of young people in religious institutions, sapping the strength and vitality of faith communities, and creating a more barren religious landscape for the young adults who do eventually decide to return to it.[1]

In the fall of 2012 the Pew Forum on Religious Life made headlines with its report that a third of American adults under the age of thirty claimed no religious affiliation, compared with only 9 percent of adults sixty-five and older. For those who had followed the polls, this finding was not entirely surprising. According to a 2007 survey of over a thousand young adults by Lifeway Research, seven in ten Protestants ages eighteen to thirty—both evangelical and mainline—who went to church regularly in high school said they stopped attending by age twenty-three. And more than a third of those said they had not returned, even sporadically, by age thirty. According to a 2013 survey by the Barna Group, 65 percent of Catholic-raised young adults say they are less religiously active today than they were at age fifteen. Even as far back as 2001, a researcher at Hebrew Union College found that the percentage of Jews who had at least two religious affiliations (a synagogue, Jewish Community Center (JCC), or other Jewish organization) was only 25 percent among those ages twenty-five to thirty-four, compared to 58 percent for those sixty-five and over. A 2012 Gallup poll found that "Americans are least religious at age 23 and most religious at age 80."

As Mark Chaves, a professor at Duke University and the author of *American Religion: Contemporary Trends*, writes, "People in the pews are getting older." Using data from the General Social Survey, he concludes that while "older people have always been overrepresented in American congregations . . . this overrepresentation has been exacerbated lately." In the 1970s, people who attended church frequently were on average three years older than the general population. In 2008, there was a five-year gap. We have reached a point where "the average churchgoing adult in the United States is now 50 years old." And when young adults do walk into a congregation where middle age is the norm, it seems unlikely they'll stay.

Some experts say that we have reason to remain calm in the face of these trends. Frank Newport, the editor of the Gallup Poll, for instance, concluded in his book *God Is Alive and Well: The Future of Religion in America* that the aging of the U.S. population may actually portend good things for the health of faith here. He notes the strong correlation between age and faith and posits, "It is a good bet that we are going to see a religious renaissance among baby boomers as they age. As a result—and as long as younger Americans don't stray from religion in huge numbers—the country as a whole will become substantially more religious in the decades ahead."

Rodney Stark, a distinguished professor of religion at Baylor University and the author of *The Triumph of Christianity*, agrees that warnings about American secularization are overblown. "I think there's an enormous amount of concern about losing these young people, and it's probably a false alarm," he tells me. "You can go back to Gallup polls in the 1930s and you find that people under the age of thirty aren't coming to church. As soon as they get married they come back." He says, with a note of frustration, "The Barna Group [which has reported on declining religious interest among millennials] has scared the heck out of people. It's caused churches to panic and to spend money they don't need to spend on things that can't be cured."

Stark cites Peter Berger, the prominent Boston University sociologist, who early in his career bought into the idea that as modernization spread, the world was headed inexorably toward secularization. About twenty years into his career, Berger began to realize that the evidence for this trend was simply not there, particularly in America. Berger once famously remarked that if India was the most religious country and Sweden the least religious, then America was a nation of Indians ruled by Swedes. Not only did this statement more accurately describe the actual religious makeup of the country, but it suggested a reason for the blinders that many academics tend to put on when thinking about religion. As part of the Swedish ruling class, they don't know anyone who goes to church—so how could we be living in such a religiously fervent country?

Berger was certainly right. American religiosity continued even as European secularization set in. But decades later, several things have changed that may make us want to reexamine his characterization.

First, religious affiliation has become more the domain of the upper classes than the working classes, as Charles Murray noted in his recent book *Coming Apart*. Writing in the *Wall Street Journal*, Murray compared the two representative towns of working-class Fishtown and upper-class Belmont: "Suppose we define 'de facto secular' as someone who either professes no religion at all or who attends a worship service no more than once a year. For the early [General Social Surveys] conducted from 1972 to 1976,

29 percent of Belmont and 38 percent of Fishtown fell into that category. Over the next three decades, secularization did indeed grow in Belmont, from 29 percent in the 1970s to 40 percent in the GSS surveys taken from 2006 to 2010. But it grew even more in Fishtown, from 38 percent to 59 percent."

How did this happen? Well, it may simply be that the ideas and habits of the elites began to trickle down to the rest of the population. Just as the social acceptance of premarital sex began with the educated classes and then became widespread among the lower classes, so it is also possible that a falling away from religion, which began with our "Swedes" at the top, has now spread to more and more of the "Indians" who make up the rest of the population.

Indeed, this seems more likely than not. Churchgoing used to be almost required in order to achieve respectability in American society. In addition to being the norm, it was also an aspirational activity. But when the upper classes decided that churchgoing was nothing but a silly bourgeois convention, it was perhaps only a matter of time before the rest of the country started dropping out. (And just as the explosion of out-of-wedlock births have had more harmful consequences to the lower classes, it is also true that the end of churchgoing for the poor has been more problematic, leading to fewer social ties and worse economic outcomes, for instance.[2])

But the real reason to wonder whether America is becoming less religious is the data on this younger generation. In 2010 the Pew Forum on Religion and Public Life published a report called *Religion among the Millennials*, in which the researchers compared this generation to other generations at the same age. Their conclusion: "Millennials are significantly more unaffiliated than members of Generation X were *at a comparable point in their life cycle* (20 percent in the late 1990s) and twice as unaffiliated as Baby Boomers were as young adults (13 percent in the late 1970s). Young adults also attend religious services less often than older Americans today. And compared with their elders today, fewer young people say that religion is very important in their lives."

The report did find that there are certain ways in which millennials have remained "traditional" in their religious views and practices. For instance, they believe in life after death and in the reality of miracles in similar percentages to older cohorts. A similar percentage even believe with absolute certainty in the existence of God. And the percentage of this generation that prays every day is also very close to that of young people in prior decades. In the 1980s it was 41 percent; in the 1990s, 40 percent; and in the 2000s, 45 percent.

But all of these measures of religiosity are extra-institutional. Praying does not necessarily mean setting foot inside a church or a synagogue or a mosque. Believing in heaven or hell does not imply anything about a particular religious group's theology. And acknowledging God's existence does not mean that you believe the same thing about God that your coreligionists do. Or even that you have coreligionists.

Atheism has not carried the day among young adults—at least not yet. Rather, a combination of agnosticism, a disinterest in and distrust of religious institutions (to which we shall return momentarily), and a general sense of confusion about exactly what we mean when we talk about religion and morality describes the current condition.

In his book *Souls in Transition*, Notre Dame sociologist Christian Smith examines the data from his vast longitudinal National Study of Youth and Religion (NYSR). The study's interviews with "emerging adults" tend to show almost no power of moral reasoning and a vague inarticulateness. Smith shows how postmodernism affects the teenage worldview.

Take this all-too-typical explanation from one respondent of how one might tell right from wrong: "Morality is how I feel too, because in my heart, I could feel it. You could feel what's right or wrong in your heart as well as your mind. Most of the time, I always felt, I feel it in my heart and it makes it easier for me to morally decide what's right and wrong. Because if I feel about doing something, I'm going to feel it in my heart, and if it feels good, I'm going to do it."

Smith notes that the persistent use of "feel" instead of "think" or "argue" is "a shift in language use that expresses an essentially subjectivistic and emotivistic approach to moral reasoning and rational argument." He concludes that such young adults "are de facto doubtful that an identifiable, objective, shared reality might exist across and around all people."

This kind of reasoning, if you can call it that, doesn't generally lead people to conclude there is or is not a deity. But this stance also doesn't motivate them to find out about, let alone become a particularly involved member of, a religious community either. With no shared reality and each one of us experiencing God differently, what do we have to learn from religion? That is where the real problems seem to arise.

According to the Pew Report, only 18 percent of millennials report attending religious services weekly or nearly weekly. That's compared to 26 percent of baby boomers and 21 percent of Generation Xers at the same age. It's not a steep drop-off but it is a steady one, says Mark Chaves. "There is a long-term pattern," he says. "Each generation is a little less religiously involved than the one before it." And he has found that no single event like the terrorist attacks of September 11, 2001, for instance, has really changed the way people practice religion in the long run.

Indeed, Chaves goes further to say there is "nothing new or unique about twenty-somethings, and it is misleading to focus on just one age group or cohort." They are just sinking down a little further than their parents on the religiosity scale.

Others, however, say this new phase of emerging adulthood is definitely presenting unique challenges. David Kinnaman, the author of *You Lost Me: Why Young Christians Are Leaving Church and Rethinking Faith*, says that technology is in part to blame for the problem. In the same way that young adults have become accustomed to taking a little bit of what they need from a variety of sources—whether it's music or online college courses—they get some of their spiritual nourishment from websites, some from a church, and some from their social group. Kinnaman explains, "They still think of and use institutions in a 'What's in it for me?' kind of way." So they take what they need. But then, he says, "Institutions are less significant in shaping and creating the entirety of their experience."

In addition to new technology and the fact that young people seem averse to joining institutions, other factors are pulling them away from organized religion. For one thing, they are responding to the new social cues we have about church attendance—which is to say, no stigma is attached to saying you don't belong to a church anymore.

Smith, who has just collected his fourth wave of data from the NSYR (men and women in their mid to late twenties), tells me, "It is simply not going to be the case that young adults will keep returning to church at the same rates. It is more acceptable to say, 'I'm not religious' or 'I'm an atheist.' And young people are more likely to say that."

Even Russell Moore, the newly installed head of the Southern Baptist Convention's Ethics and Religious Commission, has observed this trend.

In an interview published in the *Wall Street Journal*, Moore tells the story of a friend from college two decades ago, an atheist, who asked for the name of a church that wasn't very demanding of its congregation. When Moore inquired why, the friend said he needed a church to attend because he planned to run for governor some day. Moore says the story shows that in the past you had to join a church even if you had no belief because everyone else belonged. But today his friend wouldn't feel so obliged because "the idea that to be a good person, to be a good American, you have to go to church" has largely disappeared.

But the most important reason that young people are not making a commitment to institutional religion has to do with their habits of family formation. They are getting married at later ages. The average age of first marriage for women is now twenty-seven, and for men, it's twenty-nine.

Getting married, and especially having children of one's own, was once the most common impetus for joining a church or synagogue. But now more people are not marrying at all. Cohabiting used to be seen as the precursor to marriage, but now many young people see it as an alternative to marriage. According to a 2013 report from the Center for Health Statistics, "Within three years of cohabiting, 40 percent of women had transitioned to marriage; 32 percent remained living together; 27 percent had broken up."

More Americans are also delaying having children—and more are not having children at all. America's fertility rate is currently 1.93, and it has been below the replacement rate of 2.1 since the early 1970s. Even if people do get married and have children, they are doing it later, which means many of their religious habits are already formed. And fewer children means that the family is less focused and, at any rate, focused for a shorter time on the formation of the children. Families are spending fewer years using synagogue preschools or taking children to catechism classes.

Moreover, the economic downturn may have had a negative effect on marriage. A survey in 2012 of the National Association of Consumer Bankruptcy Attorneys found that its members were seeing a large increase in people whose student loan debt is making them delay starting families. As one woman mired in student loans told the *Wall Street Journal*, "How could I consider having children if I can barely support myself?"

So perhaps the solution then is just to wait (albeit a little longer than we used to) for these young people to get their financial footing, to get married, to have children. As a patient parent might say, just give them time.

Smith worries that "a lot of religious leaders have become complacent about this." He expects that "there will be a gradual trend toward fewer and fewer coming back." And then he cautions that religious leaders "should be concerned about twenty-somethings leaving *even if they do come back.*" If they return after a long time away, "they've been formed by others." This, says Smith, will cause religious institutions even greater challenges. By the time these millennials return, they will be "more consumerist in their orientation" and more shaped by "secularist propositions."

Not only are they unaccustomed to thinking in religious terms, they are out of the habit of belonging to a religious community. Fitting back in, even if they have some impulse to try, is going to be difficult.

For all of these reasons—the trends of family formation, the cultural acceptability of not belonging to a religious institution, and the steady decline in attendance that Chaves points to—it seems to me that religious leaders have every reason for concern. We are at a crucial point in terms of arresting this decline, if only this generation can be turned around.

But first we must continue to explore the underlying reasons for this trend. Some analysts say that churches themselves—not simply larger cultural factors—are to blame for these problems. As Kinnaman found in his research, young adults find themselves at odds with the church over its view of science, sex, doubt, the broader culture, and social justice. He suggests that the church has not paid very close attention to the concerns of this generation and that young men and women are bristling at the messages that the church has been offering for millennia.

Many church leaders respond that their theology cannot change simply because they are trying to reach young people who are, in Smith's words, "formed by others." But traditionalist theology is not all that grates on young people.

In fact, well-intentioned efforts by the churches themselves may also be to blame. Take teen parachurch organizations and campus ministries, which have exploded in recent decades as part of an attempt to keep young people active in religious life. Some leaders claim that these groups have altered the way that young people view worship and have changed the expectations of what belonging to a faith group entails.

This marketing to young people actually began as far back as Billy Graham in 1940s with Youth for Christ (YFC). Back then, of course, as Thomas Bergler recounts in his book *The Juvenilization of American Christianity*, Christian leaders were primarily concerned about the threats of communism and juvenile delinquency (preachers saw the two as deeply related) rather than technology and sex. But their belief that evangelizing young people was the key to solving the world's problems has remained constant.

Although the tactic may seem obvious, prior to the 1930s, as Bergler notes, churches were intergenerational affairs, with the message tailored to adults. Adolescents (there was no such thing as "teenagers" back then) were expected to absorb the same religious ideas as their parents in largely the same manner. They were expected to aspire to what Bergler calls "Christian maturity." But "between 1930 and 1950, Americans got blasted by the Great Depression, World War II, and the Cold War," and "concerned Christians launched dozens of new youth organizations in this period in the hopes of protecting young people from the evil effects of these crises and mobilizing them to make a difference in a dangerous world."

Almost a century later, these organizations have morphed into the exciting, innovative, activist organizations that dot the nation's college campuses. From Campus Crusade to Hillel to Muslim Student Associations, observers say that while these groups have succeeded in mobilizing young people, they have also made it more difficult for young people to enter the grown-up, multigenerational churches afterward. Even at Notre Dame, where Smith teaches, he says that kids who attend daily Mass get used to what he calls a "gourmet liturgy," and have trouble finding the same level of religious experience after graduation.[3]

But the problems getting young adults into the habits of religious participation do not begin with college. Rather, they start at home, with family. The well-documented phenomenon of helicopter parents has produced a generation that not only wants to put off marriage for as long as possible but also put off responsibility of any sort. Treating young men and women in their twenties as if they are children means that their presence in churches and synagogues is superfluous. If they don't show up, nothing will go wrong. The middle-aged members of the congregation will make sure everything is taken care of. Right?

Also ironic is that the very helicopter parents who are helping to produce this lackluster religious participation are the same people making their children crazy about getting good grades, honing their athletic prowess, and getting into top colleges. Faced with an overscheduled kid, a helicopter parent is much more likely to sign him up for an SAT prep class than a church youth group.

And what of the religious institutions themselves? Do they assume that, because the megachurch model worked for the baby boomers, these large institutions will continue to attract young people? They may, but for a group that is particularly suspicious of bureaucracy and slick advertising, something different could be necessary.

The kind of radical individualism and distrust of institutions that characterizes this generation has actually earned them a great deal of praise. As *New York Times* columnist David Brooks wrote recently, they are "wonderful young people who are doing good. Typically, they've spent a year studying abroad. They've traveled in the poorer regions of the world. Now they have devoted themselves to a purpose larger than self. Often they are bursting with enthusiasm for some social entrepreneurship project: making a cheap water-purification system, starting a company that will empower Rwandan women by selling their crafts in boutiques around the world."

But the kind of individualism that inspires young adults to bypass traditional institutions in favor of small, grassroots efforts can be problematic as well. The kind of à la carte existence that Kinnaman describes in which media, education, and now religion are all ingested in small bits makes it hard to produce the kind of social change that this generation would like to see. As Brooks notes in the context of the millennial efforts in the third world, "They have little faith in the political process and believe that real change happens on the ground beneath it. That's a delusion. You can cram all the nongovernmental organizations you want into a country, but if there is no rule of law and if the ruling class is predatory then your achievements won't add up to much."

It is not the case, though, that most religious leaders are complacent in the face of all this mistrust and disaffection. After traveling around the country and interviewing dozens of rabbis, pastors, priests, and imams, I perceive a sense of desperation. They feel as if they are trying a variety of different approaches but nothing seems to be working. And while they understand the importance of keeping these young people in the fold, they also have to serve the people who actually show up every week. How much time and how many resources can they devote to a generation that seems defined by its disengagement?

These leaders wonder: Is it possible to get these young people to step up and take responsibility even if they are not married or planning to have children soon? Can religious institutions treat twenty-somethings like adults even if no one else does?

The short answers are yes and yes. I asked a variety of experts in academia and different religious communities about which groups are serving this population well and which places are actually drawing in young people on a regular basis. This book reflects the results of those interviews as well as visits to the institutions with the most promising models.

Despite the amazing religious diversity of this country, the way that faith leaders describe their problems does not vary much across religious lines. The time has come to take a broad-minded, ecumenical approach to this question. Many of the structural solutions for one religious group can be adapted to work for another group.

"There will always be winners and losers" among religious institutions, as Mark Chaves cautions. A church on the upswing today could be on the downswing tomorrow. Religious institutions may even have a natural life cycle, meaning that they can only be the "hot" item for so long.

But I have tried to pick religious institutions that seem to have some staying power, a real sense of serving millennials—and turning millennials into "servants" of a larger purpose themselves. In the seven chapters that follow, I have profiled communities from a variety of backgrounds—Jewish, Mormon, Catholic, Evangelical, Muslim—and tried to figure out what challenges they faced and how they rose to meet them. While I explain some of the theological issues that govern how each one operates, I try to go beyond those issues in order to get at the organizational and social solutions that each one has adopted.

This survey of the efforts being made to bring young adults into the fold is hardly exhaustive, and readers will notice that, despite the geographic, racial, and cultural diversity represented in these chapters, they still present a somewhat skewed portrait. With the exception of a Mormon congregation in Utah and the black church in central New Jersey, most of these chapters are focused on college-educated young people. As we have discussed, this is the population where the bulk of churchgoers in America come from and so it is where the bulk of the efforts are coming from. Also, if church is "aspirational" and if the college-educated (those with a bachelor's degree now make up a third of the population between the ages of twenty-five and twenty-nine) are setting the trends for the rest of society, there is good reason to focus on this group. By changing their behavior, religious leaders may succeed in altering larger trends.

One of the reasons that American religion has remained so vibrant for so long is that our religious institutions are constantly changing, ready to adapt to the influx of immigrants, different social and economic circumstances, and new technologies.

But this new frontier seems more frightening in some ways. It is not just the view of some secular elite that American religion is losing ground. There is no reason for hysteria, but there is cause for concern. And religious leaders and parents aren't the only ones wringing their hands. Young adults themselves are feeling a little lost. So much of life until their twenties is scripted by parents and teachers that it is hard to know what to do when they get to be their own authors.

If it's true, as a pastor told me, that leaving college is like "jumping off a religious cliff," then the institutions described in this book are the parachutes softening the fall. Ideally, they're the trampolines, propelling young people to get excited about and involved again in organized religion.

1

Location, Location, Location

How the "Theology of Place" Is Plugging Young Adults Back into Their Communities and Their Churches

IF YOU WATCH ENOUGH episodes of *House Hunters, Property Virgins*, or any of the other myriad reality shows in which people search for and eventually purchase a home, you find that buyers, and especially young buyers, want three things (in no particular order): a kitchen with granite countertops and stainless steel appliances, an open floor plan, and a location within walking distance of shops and restaurants. When I began to watch these shows a few years after my own migration from the city to the suburbs of New York, I was a little surprised by how commonly this last factor was mentioned. I nearly fell off the couch when I saw a young couple demanding that their agents find them a place "within the Cleveland city limits."

I once lived in a place with my husband where you could walk to everything—the park, the dry cleaner, the independent bookstore, the coffee shop, the outrageously priced supermarket—but I never dreamed of staying there permanently. The impracticality of not owning a car, the high rents, the tiny spaces (even with an open floor plan) never appealed to me.

It turns out, though, that I am in a minority. The evidence is not merely in reality shows or among the folks in my old neighborhood who liked bringing their newborns to hip bars to hang out. As Alan Ehrenhalt argues in his book, *The Great Inversion and the*

Future of the American City, "We are living in a moment in which the massive outward migration of the affluent that characterized the second half of the twentieth century is coming to an end. And we need to adjust our perceptions of cities, suburbs, and urban mobility as a result."

A variety of reasons exist for this return to urban life. People realized that extralong commutes were cutting into their time with family, particularly when the hours of professionals were getting longer already. Lower crime rates in urban areas also made cities more desirable. But young people might also crave the kind of close-knit community that their grandparents once had. (Many say that they experienced such an environment in college.) Now, though, instead of living in close proximity to a large extended family, young people have become part of urban tribes, groups of friends who hang out together—even once they marry and have children.

Given this shift, perhaps it is no surprise that churches, particularly evangelical ones, have rediscovered their own urban roots. Perhaps the most well-known pioneer of this trend is Timothy Keller, who was asked by the Presbyterian Church in America (PCA) to start a church in New York in 1989. Today Redeemer has well over five thousand people in regular Sunday attendance. In 2001 Redeemer launched a "church planting" center, which has successfully helped to start almost two hundred churches across the country and around the world. Keller is among the most influential church leaders in America, not least because he has advocated a serious Christian engagement with the city.

In his widely consulted book, *Center City,* Keller writes, "Paul and other Christian missionaries went to great cities because when Christianity was planted there, it spread regionally (cities were the centers of transportation routes); it also spread globally (cities were multiethnic, international centers and converts took the gospel back to their homeland) and finally it more readily affected the culture (the centers of learning, law and government were in the cities)." For these same reasons, though, Christianity in America has experienced it strongest pushback in cities. Urban areas, particularly on the coasts, have gained reputations as centers of an elitist secularism, and for the second half of the twentieth century, many Christians did not see them as particularly hospitable.

But today, the faithful seem ready to engage. Here's how *Christianity Today* editor Andy Crouch described the phenomenon in a 2012 *Wall Street Journal* article:

> A new generation of church founders believes that city centers will be the beachhead of a new evangelization. While U.S. cities aren't growing as fast as overseas metropolises like Lagos or Shanghai, their renaissance since the crime-ridden 1970s is one of the cultural headlines of the last generation, and it has been accompanied by burgeoning urban congregations. On a Sunday morning in any American city the signs of change come in literal form: placards on sidewalks and corners announcing church meetings.

But now church leaders are looking to take this migration a step further. Rather than simply relocate megachurches into an urban environment, pastors are looking to entrench a new church model into American neighborhoods.

Ray Cannata came to New Orleans from a church in suburban New Jersey. He had attended Princeton Theological Seminary and then interned at a church nearby. When he finished his degree the church hired him first as an associate pastor, and then, when the senior pastor left, Cannata took his place. He describes the church as a congregation of young families with about 250 members. "It was a place where people worked long hours and they commuted really far and they were very successful." The arrangement made it difficult for the church to really build a community since many of the people weren't even in the vicinity of the church most of the week.

But even when the members were at the church or participating in church activities, the community was not a cohesive one, according to Cannata. He was trying to figure out a way to help them with the problems they did have, but the solutions only seemed to make the communal issues worse. The church, he said, "was very much program-oriented. It seemed helpful to have a women's ministry and an old persons' ministry and a singles' ministry, but then I realized that there are unintended consequences." He says he was "creating consumers by the way I was perpetuating this model."

The extent to which religious leaders want to discourage millennials from thinking of themselves as consumers of religion is a theme that came up again and again in my interviews. On the one hand, young adults seem to have a completely me-centered mind-set when they are deciding what church to join—who has the best music, the coolest pastor, the most dynamic crowd, and which is located near my house—but a big part of what they are looking for is the opportunity to serve a community. Whether these two impulses are compatible remains to be seen.

But Cannata is very clear about the problems that church consumers create for community: "I really felt like you have a women's ministry and what happens is women are hanging out with other women. They're not hanging out with men. They're getting into their particular things, which are great and a part of the body [of Christ], but that's not the whole picture of what the body ought to be. It creates people who are more selfish and a little more 'Only other women understand me.' Same thing with men. Same thing with kids."

Cannata is a tall man with a beard and mustache. He listens intently whenever his interlocutors speak. But if they don't, he could give an hourlong monologue and you might not notice. Relaxing on a leather armchair in the living room of his shotgun-style house at a busy intersection in New Orleans, he could not look more at home as he documents the problems facing American Christianity and the difficulties it must overcome to engage the next generation of young adults.

He worries that American culture is creating an individualistic rather than communal version of Christianity. "Christianity becomes a self-help program in that context. In other words, 'I'm having trouble in my marriage, so I want the church to provide me with the data that's going to help me have a better marriage,' rather than saying, 'I'm here missionally to serve' or 'I'm part of a body, part of the family. I'm here to give and to take.'"

Cannata began to rethink all of the things he was taught about church "growth"—various theories and programs about what would increase the size of a congregation. He says, "Christianity got along fine without this stuff for 1,970 years, but it's all unique to American culture and it's unique to suburbia in a lot of ways." Catering to more congregants in order to grow the congregation seemed to him a fruitless exercise. Indeed, the Faith Communities Survey from 2013 found that young adults are attracted to congregations that place a lot of emphasis on spiritual practices, not necessarily the ones that have special programs for people in their age group.

So then Cannata began to wonder about the suburban element of the equation. He was invited to interview for a position at Redeemer Presbyterian Church in New Orleans just before Hurricane Katrina hit. "I fell in love about thirty seconds after we got here," he recalls of the visit he made here with his wife. The congregation was small, and he did not form much of an impression of the church or its current leadership. For Cannata, it seemed to be all about, to borrow a phrase, "Location, location, location."

There were a lot of things Cannata wanted to do differently when he arrived to take over three months after Katrina. And thanks to the fact that there were only seventeen church members left when he showed up, he had a blank slate. He wanted a more liturgical service, weekly Communion, and a different kind of music. But most of all he wanted something that was "neighborhood-y, that had a sense of place." He had begun to think about the "theology of place." The church had to be focused, he told me, "on one geographic area and really minister to that."

The Bible is very focused on places, notes Cannata. In any passage from the Bible, he says, you are likely to be told where something occurred. While the sermons are focused on "ethical issues and morality," he thinks that the specifics are important. The Bible mentions the places, he says, "to remind you that it's an earthly thing. It happened in a place. It's not a fairy tale. It's not 'Once upon a time.'" Someone once told him that "having a theology of place is acting like the incarnation really happened." At the end of the day, says Cannata, "We believe Jesus is God in the flesh, breaking into time and place in history. And he is really there in a real place in a real time. He didn't pick Greece. He didn't pick Illinois. He picked Bethlehem." (The way Cannata talks, some might think Jesus should have come to the Big Easy instead.)

Cannata has read Jane Jacobs's masterwork, *The Death and Life of American Cities*, four times now. Her book was the first and perhaps most important critique of urban planning in the middle of the twentieth century. She called for neighborhoods to block government-led urban renewal projects and instead form their own grassroots campaigns to revitalize city life.

Cannata looked at the city of New Orleans and wondered what happened to the once dominant Catholic parishes that served the city neighborhood by neighborhood. The geographical lines drawn by the archdiocese determined what churches people attended and what religious schools their kids would go to, which served as a way of creating tight-knit communities.

Over the years the Catholic population in New Orleans has fallen off, and the Protestant churches became more and more like they are in the rest of the country. Today, they are large and they are competing with each other, trying to draw people from across the city to their pews.

Rachelle Garner grew up in a small town in Michigan. She recalls that the church she was raised in was a twelve-minute drive ("eight minutes if you hit the lights right"), but after college she and her husband moved to Montreal. They found a church they liked but it was a forty-five-minute drive from their home. "It just doesn't make sense to do that and not be able to invest in people's lives," she tells me.

That seems to be Cannata's thinking. If people come from across the city to Redeemer, he doesn't turn them away, but he does ask them if they have looked for someplace closer to them. And he emphasizes that all of the work of the church will be to serve the uptown community where it's located. The small community groups that meet weekly, he insists, will only take place within a certain radius of the church.

By becoming a neighborhood church, he believes that people will run into each other outside of church, too. And it seems to be working. Many of the parishioners I interview mention that the people they see in church are the same ones they see listening to music on Saturday nights. Or hanging out in the local coffee shops. Redeemer has created a community, but it has also created accountability. People behave a certain way when they expect they will run into their fellow churchgoers. Will Tabor, a campus minister at Tulane University, says he often sees other congregants during the week. "That is a positive." He feels as if the church has "submitted" itself to the purposes of the neighborhood.

Eileen McKenna is a violinist who moved to New Orleans with her husband, a drummer, a couple of years ago. She actually trains horses during the day and then plays music with him in the evenings. But she insists that the "church scene" is not a separate part of her life. "I see people at my church in my daily life" and at her music gigs as well.

It is probably not a good idea to build a church around a particularly charismatic pastor—what happens when he leaves?—but Cannata has so thoroughly come to embody the theology of place that it's hard to think about Redeemer's success in his absence. His love of New Orleans extends, needless to say, to its food. He has eaten at almost all of the city's seven hundred independently owned restaurants. Literally. In fact, there is a documentary film coming out about him called *The Man Who Ate New Orleans*.

Despite this, Cannata has not packed on the pounds because he also walks several miles every day. In fact, he drives almost nowhere. He lives in a historic house near the intersection of two busy streets and a short walk from a bustling district of restaurants and shops. The office of the church is a few blocks away and so are the coffee shops where he tries to write his sermons.

Marty Garner, Rachelle's husband, tells me that Cannata "does a good job of belonging to this place, contributing to it, serving it, loving it." He has become part of the Mardi Gras parade, joining something called the Krewe of the Rolling Elvi, which is essentially a group of men who dress up as Elvis for the party. They also get together at other points during the year as well to raise money for worthy causes around the city.

While the parade has a kind of wild reputation, the Elvi, and Cannata in particular, want to make sure that people understand it's about more than just a party. It's a gathering of a community. When I visited shortly after Mardi Gras, Cannata mentioned in his sermon that some people at the parade were mocking a young girl who was developmentally disabled. When the Rolling Elvi found out, they offered her a kind of personal apology, staging their own gathering and giving her "throws" (the necklaces that are offered by parade marchers to the revelers along the route).

Also, Cannata's visible presence in the community on a daily basis, says Ashley Marsh, "bridges the gap between nonbelievers and believers." Marsh, who came with her husband, Anthony, to New Orleans from Kansas City, says there are many people in

New Orleans who "do not have Christ in their lives. I think it's excellent to meet Ray as a neighbor . . . you know, a fun guy and then to know that he is a pastor."

But it is not just Cannata who is unique. It is New Orleans. In the aftermath of Katrina, the city has become a magnet for young people looking to help rebuild. Becky Otten grew up in a suburb of Milwaukee and decided she wanted to attend Tulane. She arrived with her family on August 27, 2005. The president of the university greeted the freshman class and then asked them to leave. "We'll see you in a couple of days," Otten recalls being told. Despite her parents' concerns, she did return to the city for the second semester.

Otten grew up in a very religious home. Her mother was a Quaker, and her father was from a Christian Reformed Church. The family attended the latter. She went to a school associated with that church as well until eighth grade and then a public high school. That was when she started to question her faith, or rather, she says, her church. "I felt like everyone else acted like they were perfect. It was a combination of judgment and hypocrisy. I knew there were struggles in my peers' lives and in their parents' lives, but it always came out as, 'You are not good enough. You are not Christian enough.'" Her Christian friends questioned her decision to attend public school. At the same time she was aspiring to the popular crowd in high school, which meant drinking and partying. As her behavior worsened, she felt less and less like she belonged in church. She didn't want to be part of the "hypocrisy" she saw around her.

Finally at the end of her senior year of high school, she felt things start to come together. She went on a mission trip to Juarez, Mexico. She says the group she went with was "very real about faith and that they had messed up but that was okay. I really had started to feel my sense of purpose." Otten came to school in New Orleans knowing that she wanted to be involved in community service work. The first couple of years here she did things like gut houses with her friends in the Lower Ninth Ward and act as a teacher's assistant for a fourth grade class. She didn't feel much pull to participate in religious groups on campus. But then she found Redeemer.

In that, Otten is an outlier. Most college students I've spoken with don't tend to feel very comfortable going to local churches unless there is already a critical mass of students there. The campus religious groups are much better at catering to their needs and their schedules. And they are less intimidating.

The campus minister, Will Tabor, believes that college religious leaders are not emphasizing enough the importance for students of joining a real church. He says there are "a billion reasons" why college students don't go to church. They don't want to get up Sunday mornings. They worry they won't have fun in college if they go to a church. They worry they will be condemned by churchgoers if they do have fun in college. They believe they can't ask questions in church—or have doubts about the faith. And they think church is "boring."

Tabor hosts midweek Bible studies, but he sees it as his role to get students into a "true local church." First, because the campus groups don't generally offer the sacraments, and second, Tabor believes, that is a vital part of the Christian experience. He thinks it is important for students to get to meet people from "different backgrounds" who are going through "different struggles" and "not be isolated in your little world of college students." He says he is concerned that "if you're in a college ministry you're around people who look and act and think like you, then how are you going to step into a life that's completely different [after graduation]? Are we setting them up for leaving the church? By making it so easy here in college, are we making it really hard out of college?" Many religious leaders say the answer is yes.

And not all campus religious leaders are as accommodating as Tabor is. For some (as we will see in the case of Muslim campus life) freestanding religious institutions can be seen as competition for campus faith groups. They may not always be willing to work together to create the kind of faith pipeline that could benefit the larger religious community most.

Redeemer is very close to Tulane. The congregation actually rents space from another church. It's a lovely old building with large windows that stream in light. The pews are old-fashioned wood with no cushions—not particularly comfortable. It has a cozy feel, though, or it would in most months. But there is no heat. So it can get pretty cold in the winter when the temperature dips into the forties.

But the service moves. It has a traditional liturgy with hymns played by the church's jazz band. Cannata gives a Bible-based homily but with a lot of pop-culture references and mentions of New Orleans. He stops at various points in the service to explain the significance of different elements—even Communion. A number of members come from unchurched backgrounds and many more come from nondenominational or non-Presbyterian ones. Cannata has made an effort to be ecumenical. This is not a Presbyterian table, he says, when he is offering Communion. This is a Christian table.

Tabor says he was immediately struck by the music when he first came to Redeemer. "It was amazing." He says the worship service is "high energy," but it still feels like a church service. "They're not trying to hide that." Tabor has been to churches and to campus ministry services that seem more interested in entertaining the congregants than in being a church. At Redeemer, he says, "The music is good and Ray does try to put his best foot forward. But it is also very clear that this is a church."

Tabor is right. Redeemer doesn't feel formal, but it still feels like a church. Congregants bring in coffee with them. There is a range of attire. Most of the women are dressed up, but the men seem more casual in jeans or khakis. There are some babies and toddlers and while there is a nursery, a few of the children stay and make some noise during the service.

When Becky Otten showed up in the spring of 2006, she did not immediately see a lot of college students at Redeemer. There were only a handful of people at the first service she attended. She felt the "genuine sense that people really wanted to know who I was and how I was doing." Still, for a while she didn't become a member of the church. If she missed a Sunday it "wasn't a big deal" to her. But over time her attitude changed. "I feel like I have a vested interest in being there Sunday," she tells me.

Over the course of her time in college, Redeemer became more of a priority. She began to make certain that she came not only to Sunday services but to her community group meeting on Wednesday nights. The community group has come to play a significant role in her life. She does not allow anything to stop her from attending.

After graduation, she stayed on at Tulane for a master's degree. She has since then started working at the Center for Social Innovation at the university. In her current job she helps students "find their identity as a community leader . . . combine their passions with what they're studying to create social change." And then she helps them find internships or resources to help them achieve their aspirations.

The city of New Orleans seems to be busting at the seams with social innovators, including a large contingent of Teach for America fellows and alums. The city has cut a lot of the red tape in education and new charter schools are opening up each fall, which are attracting young teachers.

There are new nonprofits popping up all the time to help get the city back on its feet. But there is also a fledgling group of people trying to start businesses. Coffee shops are filled with freelancers of all sorts working on their laptops, meeting to discuss venture capital funding. In the spring of 2012, the city saw its first tech incubator open. The program designed to support early-stage tech startups is just a sign of how much the sector has grown in recent years.

New Orleans right now is attracting exactly the kind of people that most churches would kill for. They are young, they are socially responsible, they are innovative, they are into networking, and they like community service. And they are spilling out of the pews at Redeemer. On the Sunday I was at Redeemer, I would estimate that close to 90 percent of those in the congregation were in their twenties or thirties.

When the young people at Redeemer talk about social justice, I found, they are rarely talking about political action. If the boomer generation liked the slogan "Think Globally, Act Locally," the young men and women I met at Redeemer seemed to think locally and act locally. Very locally. As Otten tells me, "Being at Redeemer makes me take a critical look at the life I'm living every single day." She tells me about one of her friends at Redeemer who found out that another one doesn't have laundry facilities in her home. So instead of letting her take all of her kids to the local laundromat, the friend invites her over to do laundry. The kids all play together. Says Otten, "I think everyone finds out how they can be that representation of God in their neighbors' lives." Another one of her friends recently went to a seminar on becoming a foster parent. She's only twenty-three.

Kim Thompson came to New Orleans originally on a mission trip. After college, she worked as an intern at Campus Crusade bringing students down to the area. Six years later, she's still here. Some of her closest friends are people she met during the rebuilding effort. She lived with the other people on the team and recalls that even a year after the storm, theirs was the only house for blocks with lights on at night. "There were no grocery stores, no McDonalds. There was nothing. It was really important to have the community of people at our house to go through the struggles of living in a devastated area and do the work we were doing. I think my faith was really in community."

Marty Garner echoes this sentiment. He says when he first came to Redeemer, he did not initially connect with anyone. He tried another church and had the same problem. Finally, he emailed Ray Cannata. "I remember feeling like I was drowning, like I was the only person in the world." They met for coffee and Cannata encouraged him to return. When he did, he fell in with a group of guys who had gone to the University of Virginia together. Garner seems surprised that although they were from wealthy suburbs of Washington, D. C., "They were nothing like the suburban rich kids that I knew."

What Garner realized, he tells me, was that "I need community around me in order for my faith to burn more brightly. Not having that made it really difficult for me to have a private faith."

Cannata has continued to resist programming at Redeemer. He says that twenty- and thirty-somethings value "authenticity." And a number of people tell me that they like the fact that Redeemer has no "gimmicks."

Cannata wants everyone at the church to feel like a full-fledged member. At other churches, he notes, there seem to be different levels. You're only really in the church if you are a part of such and such a group. He wants to avoid that, and only recently did the church even decide to have a group of "elders." These were chosen, in part, so that Cannata does not decide on his own salary and so that other financial matters are not entirely left in his hands.

Every once in a while someone will suggest having a singles' group, and Cannata rejects the idea every time—which is not to say he doesn't want the members to find their matches. When people have been dating for a while, Cannata asks them what they're waiting for. Single people do seem to feel comfortable in the church, though. A group of women—both married and single—regularly go out to lunch or dinner together. Cannata tries to acknowledge the struggles of singles without making them feel inadequate for not being married yet.

Though he doesn't want to provide specific programs for different types of people, he does feel there is value in dividing up the church of two hundred or so people into smaller groups of about a dozen people each. The community groups meet once a week in someone's home (another reason it's important that people live nearby) to discuss the biblical passage that is being read that week. (The church sticks closely to the liturgical calendar.) The Redeemer members I spoke with were generally very enthusiastic about these groups. More cross-generational exchanges take place in these groups than in the Sunday church service, and by having the meetings in people's homes rather than in the church, a greater sense exists that neighbors are welcoming each other.

Redeemer has been growing steadily since Cannata took over, and the church is now preparing for the next phase. If the church gets past 250 members or so, a group will break off and form a new church, with the associate pastor, Shane Gibson, at its helm. The new church will be in an adjacent neighborhood and its mission will be to serve *that* neighborhood.

Just as dividing up people by age or sex or marital status has its disadvantages, so can dividing them up geographically. To wit, more than one of the members I meet complain that there is not much racial or ethnic diversity in the church. The city, as everyone learned in the aftermath of Hurricane Katrina, is very much divided along racial lines. And so if you announce that your church is only going to serve a particular neighborhood, then it is only going to serve the residents of that neighborhood, even if they're mostly white.

The neighborhood where Redeemer is based is mostly middle and upper-middle class. That being said, I did go visit a couple of members at their homes on the outskirts of the neighborhoods, and the area did not look well-off. Some of Redeemer's members appeared to be gentrifying pioneers, though I'm sure they wouldn't think of themselves that way.

Perhaps the biggest problem in New Orleans these days is the crime rates. It has the highest per capita murder rate in the United States. While most of these incidents are concentrated in the lowest-income areas, there are definitely places near Redeemer where I wouldn't walk alone at night. So it is not as if the community has removed itself from the real problems the city now faces. Most neighborhoods in the city experienced destruction from Katrina to one degree or another. But for a generation that places a high value on diversity, the theology of place may be a problem.

Jessica Carey ran into Shane Gibson, Redeemer's associate pastor, one day at a park near her house and his. She was playing with her son, and it began to rain. They ran under a shelter where her son started playing with his three children. One of them was named Jude and another was named Deacon, so Carey asked whether Gibson was religious. The two chatted for about forty-five minutes, and Carey later Googled him and learned more about Redeemer.

The two met for coffee, whereupon she told him her life story over the course of two hours. Carey grew up with little in the way of religion. She went to art school in San Francisco but didn't finish. She started traveling the country working for bands, unable to figure out what she really wanted to do. And she kept running into the man who eventually became her husband. The two had a son and decided to move to New Orleans. He had a job where he could work remotely, so they found a place where the cost of living was lower than on the East or West Coasts.

When he lost his job and couldn't find another one, things started to go south. And when he got a job in Philadelphia, they separated. It was then that she met Shane. At the end of their conversation, she recalls, "He was like, 'Well, I have the answer.'" And she said, "Great. What is it?" And he said, "God."

That was not, Carey tells me, what she wanted to hear. Carey had spent the better part of the past ten years in therapy. So as little as she thought of Gibson's "answer," she says, "It was still interesting enough to have someone give me an answer. I'd been going to therapy so much. And when someone just listens to you, you think, *How do you fix your own mind with your own mind? You can't.*"

Intrigued, Carey started seeing Gibson a lot. Carey met Gibson's wife and came to their house a few times. But it was at least two months before she actually visited Redeemer. She says she had always thought of "love as [her] religion." She tells me that she knows that sounds "cheesy"—though it is probably not an uncommon sentiment among unaffiliated millennials—but when she met Gibson and Cannata and the other parishioners, she said, "That is what they embody as human beings, the way they act. You could paint any sign outside Redeemer," but what matters is the way people act. The pastors have told her that "their purpose on earth is to love other people." Carey says, "That's something almost anybody could get on board with. And I certainly do."

She started coming to church with her son regularly and asked Shane to give her a class on Christianity. She said she knew nothing "about Jesus or God." "I don't know anything about religion because I have specifically ignored it. It's still daunting." She still doesn't feel comfortable praying in front of other people and only recently started taking Communion. She says her community group is "great." "I always sit in church on Sunday, and I want to raise my hand and ask questions." But many of those are answered for her in the community group.

Redeemer has also offered her a real community. "I have eight hundred friends on Facebook, few of whom I actually interact with in real life. When you're in college, you have built-in community." But once her husband left, Carey had no one.

Her life, she says, is better now. "I've got a clean slate as far as Christianity is concerned." And she has also begun to piece together her marriage. Her husband has sought out a church near him in Philadelphia. And when he comes down to visit, the two have been counseled by Cannata and Gibson.

And now Carey is on the road to reconciliation. She expects that she and her son will be joining her husband up north in a couple of months. She seems nervous, among other things, about finding a church in her new home. "I'm not going to drive thirty minutes on a Sunday to go to church and then drive back home. That doesn't feel like this."

Carey is symbolic of two major challenges that Redeemer faces. First, as Cannata tells me, "My number-one biggest struggle in this church is mobility." It has been the same struggle for the past six years, he notes. "Last year we took in sixty members . . . That's extraordinary for a church our size. But we lost forty members because almost a third of the church moved away."

Part of the theology of place is putting down roots, says Cannata. "I want them to stay, and I have this whole big spiel I give people about why it's the greatest place in the world to live." He acknowledges that not everyone might agree, but what he wants is for people to commit to a particular place, even if it's not this place. "I'll tell somebody, honestly, if moving to Portland means you'll put down roots there and live there for the next fifty years, I'd rather have you in Portland for fifty years than in New Orleans for two and Seattle for two and Illinois for two. Go somewhere and put down roots."

And when they do, what will they find. Will there be another church like Redeemer? Another pastor like Ray Cannata? It's possible. But Carey is right to worry. Redeemer has a lot going for it, but it may not be easily replicable. For better or worse, it may be a product of its time and a place.

2

The All-American Mosque

*How Shedding Immigrant Ways Can Reshape
Islam in the United States*

CARS ARE PARKED for two blocks on either side of this well-appointed home in Santa Barbara. A mile or so from the center of town, with all of its posh oceanfront restaurants and throngs of tourists, the house seems small from the outside but it goes back deep onto the corner lot. Inside is a large gourmet kitchen and a two-story great room. When I arrive, young adults are milling around the house, offering their potluck dishes for the hostess's inspection. At the beginning of the evening, it is mostly single women in attendance, but over the course of a few hours the ratio starts to even out. About half of the women are wearing headscarves. Some are married and have small children while others are single. The men are dressed smartly in designer jeans and button-down shirts.

This is an evening sponsored by Muslims Establishing Communities in America (MECA). An organization of young adults—single, married, or married with young children—MECA was launched in 2005 by Jihad Turk, the director of religious affairs at the Islamic Center of Southern California. Though MECA is not technically a part of the Islamic Center, the center does give MECA funding for its programs. Those programs are mostly social, but they generally include a religious element as well. MECA's role is to draw unaffiliated young adults into a low-pressure religious environment and then eventually try to funnel them into mosques—and even into taking on leadership roles at Muslim institutions. The Islamic Center offers general guidelines for running those programs, but because many young adults are intimidated by the idea of a mosque and have been turned off by their experiences at mosques, the Islamic Center carefully keeps its distance.

A question for any religious institution trying to welcome young adults into the community is whether to give them their own organization or to integrate them fully with other generations. MECA exists as its own entity, but it is meant to serve as a pipeline, especially for young leaders, to become a part of the Islamic Center eventually. Other institutions like Redeemer in New Orleans are totally multigenerational (or they are open to any generation, anyway). Some try to provide a separate space for young adults but also include them in the whole community, as we will see in subsequent chapters.

Religious leaders are faced with the question of how to welcome these young adults, to make institutions seem less stodgy, while showing the continuum of religious life, exposing young men and women to older mentors as well as young people who will look up to them. How do you give them a separate space and show them that there is more to their spiritual stories than just this one chapter? It is a delicate balance, but MECA's model is showing signs of success.

Before people settle down for the meal at this event, most of the men and a few of the women go into another room to recite evening prayers. But many people continue to socialize and try to keep the children's voices down until the prayer is over.

Dinner is buffet style with platters of food practically spilling off the table. Everyone ends up with a mishmash of traditional dishes from Pakistan, the Middle East, and North Africa, along with pizza and sandwiches.

When dinner is winding down, Turk asks everyone to move toward the living room. There are pillows scattered on the floor and some chairs along the walls. People try to find seats. Some go upstairs where a small balcony accommodates a few more. Women and men are mostly sitting on opposite sides of the room. Turk welcomes the attendees and then offers a "Koranic reflection." He tells the gathering that the Koran is "accessible to each of us without a scholar." Yes, he says, there is a need for scholars of the tradition, but those scholars cannot stand between a Muslim and the Koran.

It's not quite Martin Luther nailing his Ninety-Five Theses to the wall, but one senses that for some in the room, this is a refreshing new approach to the faith. And they listen intently as Turk reads a verse: "Let there arise out of you a group of people who stand up for doing good. They join in the good and forbid the wrong."

Then he asks the assembly, which has now grown to well over one hundred people, to consider their reaction to these verses—"What do I feel? What do I think?"—and share their answers with the group. He tells them not to ask questions of himself or of those around them. "And don't quote someone else in your answer," he adds emphatically.

Slowly, some answers start coming. One man says the passage makes him "feel inspired to seek social justice." Another says it makes "religion seem easier." A man says that the passage reminds him of what is happening in Syria—"There are people standing up to a repressive regime." And he suggests that Americans are to be praised for supporting the Arab Spring, while Middle East dictators are not "joining in the good."

Turk tries to draw more people into the discussion, calling on both women and men to offer their ideas. He tries to prevent the people who seem more familiar with the passage from dominating the conversation.

He thanks everyone for their participation, and then various members of the group start to make announcements about upcoming events—a hiking group, a biking group, a coffee group for recent converts, a health fair. Someone gets up to ask for volunteers to come to the Islamic Center's food pantry, which is open on Saturday mornings. Turk talks about a trip he is leading in a few months to "Palestine and Israel" with a "mixed group of Muslims, Jews, and Christians."

He concludes the announcements with a broader call to get involved in the organization. "MECA should be welcoming to people of all backgrounds," he says. "There is no agenda for this group." He wants people from different backgrounds to get together and "talk about something meaningful."

At around 9 p.m., the last formal part of the evening program commences. Turk divides the assembly into smaller discussion groups with about a half dozen people each. He asks them to think about the question, "What is the role of the mosque?" He instructs them to consider the broad categories of "spirituality, education, the formation of an American-Muslim culture, community, and service."

As I listen in, the members of my assigned discussion group talk about the importance of the mosque in "helping the needy, regardless of their faith," "pulling in more young Muslims," "providing more opportunities for the young and the elderly to engage," and "broadening the types of activities the mosque sponsors." They have ideas for more community service activities, like reading to kids from low-income families or building a house through Habitat for Humanity. And they want to see how the mosque can "make spirituality relevant to young people," help them cope with "peer pressure and stress." They want a religious education at a mosque to "include education about other faiths."

When the discussion groups disband, Turk asks a representative of each to stand up and give a summary of their findings. Almost all of the volunteers are female, which might seem unremarkable in another context. Turk can't help but joke that "women are large and in charge on this."

An outsider listening to these exchanges both on the Koranic text and the role of a mosque could easily mistake them for somewhat elementary discussions—maybe among high school or college students—about forming a new club or encountering a religious text for the first time. It's not that the young adults there—mostly between the ages of twenty and thirty—weren't mature or intelligent. Rather, this is new territory for many of them. Not many Islamic religious leaders have ever asked their opinions on these matters before.

For one thing, among those who received a religious education growing up, interpretation of texts was not really part of the program. Most Muslim educators simply require that young people memorize passages in Arabic and (sometimes) translate them.

Meymuna Hussein-Cattan's parents came to Southern California from Ethiopia when she was three. She didn't go to Friday prayers regularly because she was in school, but she attended Sunday school in Orange County. "As far as the Koran, I think there was more emphasis on memorizing than on understanding or comprehending," she tells me. "I wouldn't say that I looked at the Koran intellectually until a couple of years ago." Hussein-Cattan recalls learning how to pronounce words in Arabic but never learning what they meant.

For many young men and women like Hussein-Cattan, the holes in their religious education came to light when they went to college. There they studied texts—even texts that were originally written in other languages—with a critical eye. And they began to wonder why the Koran could not be read and understood the same way.

Homaira Shifa's parents and grandparents fled Afghanistan when the Soviet Union invaded in 1979. When Shifa was growing up, there were few Islamic institutions near her home in Southern California. Her parents worked two, sometimes three jobs each in order to make ends meet. And her grandparents mostly raised Shifa and her siblings. "They taught us what they knew themselves," she tells me. "They knew verses in the Koran they had memorized. . . . They wanted to teach their grandchildren and pass on their wisdom."

But their version of Muslim wisdom left Shifa and her siblings confused. "We'd pray five times a day and we'd recite certain verses in our prayers, and we wouldn't even know what it meant. You know? That's when my brothers and I were asking, *What does it mean? What are we doing?*"

This problem might feel familiar to Jews of a certain generation. Many children and grandchildren of Jewish immigrants grew up learning how to "read" Hebrew, but never understood either the prayers they were reciting or the passages from the Torah that were chanted each week before the congregation. Hundreds of thousands of children have gone through years of Hebrew school to come out knowing only the most basic words and no real sense of what the texts of the tradition mean.

For many Muslims and Jews, this situation has led to a certain kind of alienation from their faith. If learning to be fluent in Arabic is the precursor to understanding what is going on at their religious institutions, then it is unlikely that many of those religious institutions will thrive. Many Jewish institutions have come to the same conclusion with regard to Hebrew. Their reactions to this problem have come in two forms. Reform synagogues hold services mostly in English. Meanwhile, Conservative and Orthodox Jews have tried to engage in a much more comprehensive language program. Jewish day schools now offer Hebrew language immersion rather than simply a haphazard collection of words and grammatical rules every year. At the same time, they are also trying to teach children the meaning of the prayers they are reciting and encouraging discussion of the Torah and rabbinical texts in English.

Perhaps it seems obvious to say, but in order for a religious institution to attract young adults in America, it has to be sufficiently American, which is not to say that it can't be somewhat countercultural or that its leaders cannot hold more traditional views about marriage and family. It is simply to say that young adults are creatures of the culture in which they were raised. The acronym MECA is no accident. These are young adults establishing communities *in America*. The name implies not only a certain break with the "old country" that many American religious groups must accommodate but also a sense that certain things about the ideals of equality and freedom in the United States make it particularly appealing to young people.

From the perspective of a Muslim leader in America, Shifa turned out just fine. Rather than rebel against her tradition, Shifa decided to become a more active participant. She joined a Muslim group in high school, where she started to get more exposure to the meanings of her tradition. And when she went to college, she started to engage with it more intellectually. "Once I understood the meaning, that's when I fell in love with it more. I embraced it a lot more once I knew what I was saying." But Shifa may be the exception.

According to Pew, there are about 2.8 million Muslims in the United States, and 63 percent are immigrants. Large waves of Muslim immigrants arrived here in the 1980s—some people refer to this as the "student era." As Mazen Hashem, a lecturer in sociology at the University of Southern California, tells me, "Many immigrants came in as students and they weren't sure they would stay. But as things turned worse in their home countries, they decided to remain in America. They thought, *Well, it's not so bad. I'm living in this country as a Muslim.* They got married and had kids here. Going back after that is complicated."

But like many generations of immigrants before them, they did not want to give up their culture and traditions. Since many of them came here as young adults, their formative years had already been spent in Pakistan or Egypt or Lebanon. So the families they started and mosques they formed here reflected their cultural preferences as much as their religious ones. They spoke the language, ate the food, wore the dress, and practiced the same kinds of cultural traditions as their former countrymen, and in many cases they assumed that their children would, too.

Soha Yassine was born in Beirut, Lebanon, and came here with her parents when she was one year old. Her father, she tells me, also considered moving to Saudi Arabia where he had worked for a time, but decided "you can't raise girls there." Yassine was brought up without much knowledge of Islam at all. She was fifteen the first time she went to mosque. "I didn't even know the name of the Prophet Muhammad. I thought his name was Muhammad Ali, but it turns out he's a boxer."

But Yassine did not have a typical American upbringing either. "I was raised Arab," she tells me. "Growing up, my parents would say things like, 'We don't do that. We're Arab.' Or 'This is not okay for you as an Arab girl.'" Though her parents wanted her to be educated, they were very traditional about their attitudes toward women.

This tension between cultural and religious identity has a long history in America. Culture is a kind of easy entry point for people into religious communities. Surrounded by the language and food and music of their parents and grandparents, some young adults find themselves at home in more traditional religious institutions. It can be a kind of comfortable retreat. But the kind of questioning or even rebellion that accompanies adolescence and young adulthood also produces a desire to understand the religious principles that are supposed to underlie cultural practices. That questioning can lead young people to leave a religious community altogether, or it can mean that they attempt to strip away some of the cultural wrapping and focus more on faith itself.

As many American immigrant groups have found, culture and religion are difficult to separate, and older generations have trouble trying to explain to their children what is so important about religion outside of the context of their immigrant culture.

Over time, Yassine became less and less concerned with what Arabs do and more and more interested in what Muslims do. She went to an Islamic high school, where she learned Arabic. She got a rigorous secular education as well, taking AP classes and eventually earning admission to the University of California, Los Angeles (UCLA). She said it was at her Islamic school that she "began meeting educated Muslim women. I didn't know they existed. I really thought that they were all oppressed and subservient to their husbands." She recalls seeing the movie *Not without My Daughter*, in which Sally Field plays an American woman trapped by her Iranian husband in Iran permanently after they go on what is supposed to be a short trip there. "I thought that was real," Yassine tells me. "Or I thought that was how Islam stood on women." But then she met "these principals and teachers, all these empowered, awesome, amazing, educated women." High school was, in her words, "an intellectual and spiritual revolution."

Yassine has come to believe that the oppression of women in Muslim societies is cultural, not religious. And so she is turned off by many of the American Muslim institutions that insist on segregating women from men or treating them poorly. She says despite her religiosity in high school, she never found a spiritual home in college. She found the Muslim Student Association's "approach to gender very weird." They were "not friendly to women." She continued to pray the five daily prayers all through college, but she "didn't find a place there."

Jihad Turk confirms the impression of many of the young men and women I interview. Most American mosques, he says, "seem like old boys' clubs." "There is one man [here]," says Turk, referring to a member of the leadership at the Islamic Center of Southern California, "who has been here since 1953." He says mosques are "masculine-dominated. It's usually a bunch of uncles who all know each other." The term "uncle" is used to signify any older man who is not your father. "It becomes like a cultural oasis from back home, and the kids don't share that same culture exactly."

Their children and grandchildren feel more American and say they are stifled by religious communities dominated by the rules of a particular culture. Even those I speak to who are more religiously oriented say they care more about the faith than about cultural traditions brought over from the old country. These sentiments echo those of America's previous waves of immigrants— Irish Catholics and Italian Catholics or German Jews and Russian Jews who, after a generation or two in the United States, stopped drawing the ethnic distinctions of their parents and grandparents.

In his book *Protestant, Catholic, Jew*, published over sixty years ago, sociologist Will Herberg predicted that the distinctions among different ethnicities would disappear in America. Italian Catholics and Irish Catholics would, after a generation or two, start to overlook their country of origin, even while they clung to their Catholic faith. Polish Jews and German Jews would do the same. In this way, Americans would become a country of large religious groups whose ethnic differences wouldn't be of much consequence.

Muslims seem bound to be caught in that same process. Their children do care about the faith but they find their elders' focus on ethnic differences to be irrelevant, if not backward. (A similar attitude can be found among young people in the Eastern Orthodox Churches. The adult children of Greek or Armenian immigrants are not fluent in the languages of their parents' home countries, and leaders in those churches have noticed a drop-off in attendance among the younger generation.)

There is an extent to which being "ethnic" is cool in America today. The embrace of cultural diversity means that young Muslims may find their particular food or language (or some forms of dress) to be welcome additions to college campuses or young adult communities. Religious leaders may be able to draw young people to Muslim events or mosques with some of this ethnic fare and holiday celebrations. But the cultural norms that have followed their parents from the Middle East or North Africa are an entirely different story.

And Muslim young adults have, to some extent, come to

believe that it is cultural prohibitions and traditions from the old country—not the theological dictates of Islam—that are preventing their community from becoming more modern and more American.

This is particularly true with regard to the role of women in Islam. In the workplace and in school, Muslim men and women have regular interactions with members of the opposite sex. But in Muslim institutions, prayer, education, and social events are all segregated by gender. It's a disconnect that bothers many of the young adults I speak with.

In addition, many of the Muslim women would like to be able to take a more active role in Muslim institutions. Islam in America might benefit if they did. Without getting into a theological debate about how the Koran sees women, sociologically speaking, women have an essential role to play in American religion. They are more likely to attend religious services regularly, more likely to volunteer in various capacities at religious institutions, and more likely to be in charge of children's religious upbringing. According to a survey I conducted in 2010, children of interfaith marriages are more than twice as likely to be raised in the religion of their mother. Religious institutions in America that do not take account of these facts do so at their own peril.[4]

But many of the MECA women I've spoken to tell me that one reason they don't feel comfortable at so many mosques they have visited is because of their attitude toward women. Meymuna Hussein-Cattan tells me that she did not grow up wearing a hijab, and her impression is that the East African communities are generally more liberal about things like women's dress and women being able to dance in public.

But most mosques take a stricter view. "My problem with the mosque," she tells me, "is actually how women police each other." She describes to me an incident a few years ago during Ramadan when she went into a mosque quickly because she did not want to be late for prayers. "Instead of being greeted with respect and welcoming, I was actually reprimanded for not having a hijab on. [That] was the first thing this woman noticed." The other women nearby did not "see anything wrong with that interaction. They thought it was fine that she could talk to me like that."

And it's not just women who find the attitudes of most Muslim institutions to be backward. Shukry Cattan, Meymuna's husband, tells me one reason he rarely goes to a mosque is "because I want to be able to pray with my wife by my side and I can't do that in any mosque, even the Islamic Center." Even with the enlightened views about the role of women and their ability to discuss and master religious texts, women at the Islamic Center must pray in a separate section of the mosque, behind all the men.

Some people tell me this is the only practical solution to the fact that women (for reasons of modesty) do not want to be kneeling and lying prostrate with men directly behind them. But still, it seems to be a barrier to young adults feeling comfortable in the mosque.

In graduate school, Soha Hassine continued her intellectual study of the Islamic tradition. But she still did not find a community where she felt comfortable. At one point, she found herself living in Boston with no Muslim friends around. With no community, she says, "I felt like my practice was becoming very superficial. I was just wearing a hijab, but how Muslim am I?"

She was having some difficulty studying Islam, too. "Whenever you take an academic approach to studying any faith tradition, it inevitably challenges you. You can sink or swim. So I really needed the support to be able to deal with these new questions."

She had heard about MECA and was very excited about the "great group of young professionals who could hang out and be friends, but also continue to learn about Islam." She says that "a lot of time, when you come to the mosque, there are old people there and they're not concerned with issues that are relevant to us." Soon after she began attending MECA events, she joined the group's leadership.

When she thinks about what would attract people in their twenties and thirties to Muslim institutions, she comes back to the attitudes of the leadership toward women, members of other religions and races, and people with other sexual orientations.

She says she won't go so far as to call the mosque leadership's attitude "misogyny," but she notes, "They're not empowering women or as supportive of women as they should be." And she also thinks that young Muslims are turned off by "homophobic preachers." "Yes, as Muslims we don't accept homosexuality," she acknowledges, but "that is not a green light to be homophobic or spread hate or otherize people." She says the Islamic Center is a "breath of fresh air from all that."

The attitude of evangelical Christians toward homosexuality has been liberalizing in recent years. A 2011 Pew Poll found that almost half (44 percent) of young evangelicals between the ages of eighteen and twenty-nine favor allowing gays and lesbians to marry. Among the evangelical population as a whole, only 20 percent favor it.

Previous generations of Christians espoused a "hate the sin, love the sinner" approach, but many young adult Christians have also adopted the idea that homosexuality may have a biological basis and as a result it is not something that can really be "blamed" on gays and lesbians. Regardless, they say, there is no reason to be "hateful" in the condemnation of homosexual behavior.

My conversations with young adult Muslims have led me to believe that they have formed a similar attitude. Even if they accept the religious prohibition on homosexual behavior, they find the cultural attitudes about its practice to be backward or "bigoted."

In the same vein, they tend to have more enlightened attitudes (they say) than their elders about members of other religions and members of other cultures. As for the former, they tell me they would like to understand better what Christians and Jews believe, for instance. And, as they noted during the MECA discussion, they think it is the role of the mosque to teach them about other religions and to partner with other religious institutions. Many members mention to me the importance of embracing "diversity" in their lives.

Attendance at MECA events is not meant to replace attendance at a mosque, but it is a solution to the mosque's most pressing problem—a dearth of young adults in attendance and an almost complete absence of young adults in leadership positions. Observers outside the Muslim community tend to focus on its potential for radicalization. But the Muslim leadership knows that they must pay attention to a much larger trend.

The story of Islam in America today is a story of rapid assimilation and even secularization. Jihad Turk says that of the roughly 750,000 Muslims living in Southern California, just 30,000, or about 4 percent, regularly attend Friday prayer.

Many of the young adults I've spoken to say they have disaffected friends who have fallen away from the faith. Mosque attendance is not the only measure of religious observance, but Muslims are experiencing other signs of secularization as well. They are intermarrying at rates comparable to those of other religious groups in America. The Pew Forum on Religion and Public Life estimates that about one in five Muslims is wedded to someone of another faith.

In part, this is simply the story of religion in America. After the first generation arrived, their children realized that religion was a choice here. This is not a majority Muslim country. There is no government telling you to conform to the faith, as is often the case in Arab countries. And Muslims in America do not experience the kind of geographical isolation that often occurs in European countries. There are places like Dearborn, Michigan, with a higher concentration of Muslims, but there is nothing like the Muslim ghettos surrounding Paris. Finally, recent surveys show an increasing number of religiously unaffiliated Americans as well as a high number of "religion switchers." Muslims in America are not exempt from these trends.

According to Turk, the challenge of Los Angeles' Islamic Center, in its view, is to help American Muslims assimilate without betraying the tenets of Islam. "How do we carry forth the charge to speak for truth . . . and live life based on a moral foundation?" Turk asked his congregation during one Friday prayer session. "If we find ourselves caught up in the rat race, we won't have fulfilled our religious commitment."

Turk's message is one that was deeply related to American life. He began with American history, noting that as many as 30 percent of the slaves who were brought here centuries ago were Muslims. "They were prevented from passing on their faith." Then a generation of Arab immigrants came here in the early twentieth century. They, too, failed to pass on their faith. Turk asks how this last wave of immigrants, those who came here in the latter part of the twentieth century, can avoid the same fate.

He tells those gathered to be vigilant when it comes to bringing up their children in the faith. "At a certain age, children become more influenced by their friends than their parents." He advises parents to have dinner with their children, to "open the channels of communication," and to model religious rituals for them. "Do daily prayers together as a family. Let that be a sweet moment for you."

Muslims in America are better off economically than the average American. Since the ones who immigrated here typically came with student visas, they are college educated and have made provisions for their children and grandchildren to follow in their footsteps. They have used their wealth to construct a great many mosques. Turk estimates that there are 120 mosques in Southern California alone. But he worries that these will be "buildings of great emptiness" if younger Muslims lose their religious identity.

He warns those assembled to keep close watch over their children's choice of friends. "You will find good friends among both Muslims and non-Muslims," he says, warning parents that just because a friend is Muslim doesn't mean he's a good influence on your child.

But even all of this vigilance is not enough, says Turk. "We need to start being concerned about college and postcollege," he explains. He is worried about the high rates of interfaith marriage. "When they marry out, they drift away." MECA, he tells them, is a way to fight back against this trend.

Ahlam (who only wanted her first name used) grew up Muslim in Southern California and says she didn't start practicing Islam until she was in college at San Diego State. She has found many of the mosques she has been in too strict, and she sees their mostly foreign-born and educated leaders as off-putting. Often they simply don't have any messages that are relevant for younger Americans. They repeat the same Friday sermons, known as Khutbahs, week after week. As Ahlam tells me, "There are only so many times I want to hear the hadith about how smiling is a kind of charity."

While she found a group of likeminded coreligionists in college, the transition afterward was difficult. "I wanted to linger on campus after graduation. I went to Islamic Relief events there. I wanted to continue that relationship." But eventually she tried to find a community of Muslim adults with whom she felt comfortable. It wasn't easy.

Turk notes the large attrition rate for young Muslims. He says that many of the mosques he is familiar with are trying "to figure out ways to bring their kids back after college. Our kids are going off to college and then they don't plug back into the community."

One reason may have to do with the Muslim college experience itself. The most visible Muslim presence on most college campus is the Muslim Student Association (MSA). But many recent alumni report that their involvement in the MSA had more to do with political activism than any kind of religious connection. Shukry Cattan tells me that he joined the MSA at UCLA, but it was "because they did a lot of political work, especially around Palestine and Iraq. That was where my connection was. It had nothing to do with spirituality."

According to sociologist Mazen Hashem, being Muslim on campus "is more of a social identity. The religion is part of it. But there is at the same time a feeling that we need a group." He says to the extent that religious leaders even pay attention to the younger generation of Muslims, they are trying to draw them to mosques off campus rather than provide some kind of prayer or religious services. The services they are willing to provide are typically for the very young or families. "There's still a big gap in our community where you have the teenage years." For the mosques, he says, it is not "a priority."

MECA is seen as a welcome alternative to many of the Muslim young adults living in the area. And there are Muslim leaders from other areas of the country who are trying to replicate it. Its president, Jahan Hamid, is an airline pilot and has contacts in cities across the country, and he is trying to coordinate efforts in Phoenix and New York, among other places.

Hamid grew up in Norway and received most of his religious education at home. He moved to the United States at the age of twenty just a few weeks before 9/11, and like many Muslims of his generation, that event made him want to find other Muslims with whom to associate. "I found myself in a situation where I needed some sort of a community of support because there were so many questions—especially in my field of aviation." He says he was initially "very hesitant to go to the mosque" because of the "perception of people at the time."

He eventually found MECA. Some friends of his asked him to go to a picnic for MECA. "The welcome that I got was just open heart and open arms. It was amazing." He remembers going to a potluck event shortly thereafter. "I walk in and the first thing I get was a big hug. It was like, *Wow, I never had this.* There was so much love." He liked the idea that MECA was "low pressure, low intensity." The attitude of the leaders was "Come on, sit down, have some good food together." They showed a movie and had a little Koranic reflection, and then there was just mingling. "I found that to be so comfortable. You know, I felt like I'm not alone anymore."

When Hamid talks about why he likes MECA, mostly what he talks about are the things that make the group fit in well in America. He likes the fact that ethnic differences don't matter as much at MECA. His family is Pakistani and his fiancée's family is from Afghanistan, but this does not cause problems for anyone at MECA. Hamid likes the fact that MECA and the Islamic Center have interactions with other faith groups, and he likes the fact that MECA members do community service, interacting with people of all backgrounds through their food pantry and other volunteer activities.

One of MECA's newest ventures is trying to deradicalize the prison population. He and his friends in MECA worry that prisoners are often given material on Islam in prison that is not accurate. They send what they see as more truthful material to prison libraries and answer letters from prisoners about the tenets of Islam.

Hamid likes the hands-on community service that members of MECA perform—including the food pantry. More than one person tells me that the older generation sees charity in a financial light while the young adults more often volunteer their time. Says Soha Yassine, "The older generation is much more willing to cut a check for ten thousand dollars. The younger generation doesn't have that kind of money. So what else can we do but volunteer our time and services?" In her experience with MECA, she has noticed, this demographic will use "their experience, their Western educations, their Western modes of organizing to drive those programs forward."

There has always been a temptation for immigrants to want to keep their religious traditions, but in an era when young adults are moving away from affiliation with religious institutions anyway, it is all the more important that those institutions find a way to adapt to this country by grounding themselves in American traditions. They needn't give up on their religious beliefs, but they must figure out how much of their practice is the result of an immigrant experience and how much is actually derived from tenets of the faith. If history is any guide, ethnic identities do not survive for long in this country, but religious traditions can.

3

Joining the Service

*How the Catholic Church Is Training a New Generation
of Laypeople to Be Spiritual Leaders*

WHEN LEADERS OF the Catholic Church talk about a demographic problem they are not usually talking about a dearth
of young adults in the pews. That's an issue, too, of course. But the
Catholic Church is facing a more urgent crisis. There are fewer
and fewer nuns, priests, and brothers to minister to the faithful.
While the overall population of Catholics in the United States
grew by more than 8 percent every decade from 1950 to 2000
(in more recent years due to immigration), the number of priests
decreased by 13 percent for each ten years and the number of
people in religious orders decreased by 20 percent. Today, one in
seven parishes in the United States no longer has a resident priest.

And not only the parishes are suffering—Catholic institutions
from soup kitchens to schools to hospitals now must depend on
laypeople to do the jobs that clergy once assumed. In 1920, 92
percent of Catholic school staffs were made up of members of
religious orders. Today, that number is 4 percent. It is not merely
that the church can no longer depend on free labor to keep up
its institutions—though the fact that it can't has not helped the
church's troubled finances. It is also leaves open questions such
as: Where will the church's leadership come from in the future?
Are laypeople going to step into these roles? And who is training
young people to take over the spiritual and administrative responsibilities of the church?

There are well over two hundred Catholic colleges in the United States, and while some have all but abandoned their religious missions, many are still dedicated to the church. Administrators at these schools speak regularly about their commitment to the Catholic social justice tradition, and young people are deeply attracted to this idea. In part, it seems as though the church's message of service to the poor and its exemplars of self-sacrifice from Dorothy Day to Mother Teresa seem ready-made to appeal to this generation of young adults.

How much of this service ethic is sprouting intrinsically from young adults and how much of it comes from being trained by their teachers and parents to use this language is hard to determine. After all, this is really the first generation of Americans for whom service projects were an academic requirement, something to brag about on college applications.

Regardless, opportunities to exercise "social justice" seems to be something that colleges want to offer young people, too. Most secular colleges have adopted service programs; students can spend spring break volunteering for Habitat for Humanity projects or in local homeless shelters. But, interestingly, many students seem specifically attracted to Catholic colleges because of the importance they place on service. Real differences exist between secular and many Catholic colleges. For one thing, at a Catholic school the service is placed in the context of the faith, with prayers or religious messages offered as part of the volunteer work; also, a significant number of Catholic college graduates actually do some kind of service full-time after graduation.

At Notre Dame, somewhere between 10 and 12 percent of the senior class goes into service after graduation. In the early 1990s, some faculty and administrators at the university began to notice that very few of these students were going into Catholic education. Indeed, some of them were heading off for programs like Teach for America, but it wasn't just urban public schools that needed help. It was urban Catholic schools. So they decided to start a pilot program to see which students might be interested in going into impoverished areas to teach at Catholic schools.

At the first informational meeting, 250 students showed up. They had to switch the meeting to a larger classroom, according to Father Lou DelFra, a professor at Notre Dame. Twenty years later, the Alliance for Catholic Education (ACE) has trained over twelve hundred Catholic schoolteachers and more than two hundred Catholic school leaders. Its competitive admissions program draws participants from a variety of Catholic colleges. The alliance has sent students to underserved schools all over the country. It has launched international initiatives in Chile, Haiti, and Ireland as well.

When ACE was founded, though, according to Father DelFra, it wasn't simply to be a teacher training program like Teach for America. "It was born out of this recognition that the number of religious vocations was declining in our church and we need to invite laypeople into deeper ministry, but we also need to prepare them." As he tells me, "You can't just say to the laypeople, 'Okay, now you do it and we're not going to spend any time teaching you how.'" There was the notion that ACE "can be the lay version of a religious order. [We were] preparing them to become teachers and principals and at the same time cultivating their prayer life."

The program was a great success, not only in the sense that it brought qualified teachers into the classrooms of underserved schools. It also had a deep effect on the religious lives of its participants. The program started off as only one year but then became a two-year program in which the teachers earn a master's degree, too. During their teaching stint the participants also share living quarters with others in the program and immerse themselves in Catholic life.

For many of the participants, the experience was akin to becoming a missionary, not in the sense that they spent their days proselytizing, but rather in the sense that they became part of a new community and tried to figure out ways to serve that community that were in keeping with the mission of the church. While many young adults are interested in service or volunteering once a week or a few times a year, some programs like ACE could be described as intensive service. Not only are participants supposed to work full-time in a kind of public service role at ACE, they are also supposed to live "in community." These programs seem to have a profound effect on the way young people practice their faith after college.

ACE is not the only such program. Another is the Urban Catholic Teacher Corps, run by Boston College and the Archdiocese of Boston. For those who don't want to go into education, there are also a variety of programs, including the Jesuit Volunteer Corps, typically a one-year program in which participants serve the poor or disadvantaged. Young men and women work for a nonprofit agency or the church. Depending on their skills, they can help with legal matters like immigration paperwork or work in a medical capacity or in a school.

People who do this kind of intensive service often go into other, unrelated professions afterward, but they are profoundly impacted by these experiences in their early twenties. They may end up in corporate law or investment banking. They may go to medical school or get a PhD, but they seem to retain both the longing for a religious community and the habits of belonging to one.

Megan Adzima grew up in a Catholic family in Connecticut. She went to Mass regularly as a child but after confirmation, things just "sort of petered out." She attended Villanova, a Catholic University in Pennsylvania. She didn't participate in campus ministry but she did go on a couple of mission service trips and participated in Big Brothers, Big Sisters. With a degree in Spanish and English, she wasn't sure what she wanted to do after college, and the volunteer coordinator encouraged her to apply to ACE.

In the interview with the program's coordinators, she was asked about her faith life. She still remembers her reply: "I'm really inspired by people who have strong faith lives." She explained,

"When I see my classmates going to Mass without their parents telling them to, that was something inspiring to me, something I thought I could learn from." Faith, she said, "was something I wanted to grow into."

When she attended her first meeting for ACE on Notre Dame's campus six months before she began teaching, she remembers being surprised by the religiosity of some of the other participants in the program. That weekend, she recalls, she attended Mass seven times.

Then she moved to Jacksonville, Florida, to do her teaching stint. There, Adzima says, she "tried to find my place by following the example of others." She recalls, "There was a minister at the high school who worked really hard to foster the spirituality of the students and the faculty." She taught Spanish and religion and says that she ended up learning a lot herself. "There were many times when I was humbled when the kids would ask me questions." She might not have known the answers on the spot, but she researched them and found out.

At the end of her two years, Adzima was asked to stay on and help a friend who had become a campus minister at the high school. Throughout her time, she says, she would reflect on how the program did exactly what she had hoped it might in terms of helping her grow in her faith by getting to watch others. "I think it's a beautiful thing for kids to reflect on their lives and define their identity and their own faith life."

This theme came up again and again in my interviews. The years after college are really the first time that students are faced with the issue of "defining" their identity and their faith life. For some, this can be deeply intimidating, causing them to steer away from organized religion entirely. But for others who have been through a program like ACE or who have gone on a mission with the LDS Church especially, this period can be a tremendous opportunity. It is a time when young adults really "own" their faith.

Adzima has stayed in the field of education ever since, first going to teach in Chile and now working for the Inner City Scholarship Fund, helping with Hispanic outreach. She is living in Boston but is not at all sure she wants to settle there permanently. She hasn't found a parish and is "not necessarily looking to become involved in one." Instead, she has found the Advocates for Catholic Schools, a kind of alumni program for ACE. The group holds a Mass and dinner once a month. Participants do service activities occasionally, like helping families fill out applications for Catholic schools. And once a year, during Lent, they go on a retreat together. There are close to thirty such "alumni" groups now, organized regionally, across the country.

On a chilly Friday afternoon in early March, about two dozen members of the Boston group gather at the Glastonbury Abbey in a woodsy suburb south of the city. Some of those who come are old friends. Others are new members. But they all look relieved after a long week to be coming to a place that, though unfamiliar, feels like home. After picking one of the spartan rooms to drop their backpacks and duffle bags, they wander back into the main gathering area. With fraying carpet and big windows that look out onto the country road, the attendees, almost all in their mid-twenties, start to catch up. It feels like a college reunion or even a gathering of college friends to celebrate someone's wedding.

Some of the people are still working for Catholic schools. Some are lawyers; others are in graduate school. Some are stay-at-home mothers. A few of them are married or engaged, but most are single. Not everyone here went through ACE. Some did the Urban Catholic Teacher Corps. Others participated in the Jesuit Volunteer Corps. In addition to Father Lou DelFra, who is there as the spiritual leader of the retreat, Notre Dame has also sent another young woman to be an accompanist on the keyboard for all of the hymns the group will sing over the next twenty-four hours.

We sit in a circle, and after an opening prayer different people volunteer to do short readings. The theme of the weekend is "servant leadership," a philosophy based on the model of Christ that puts the needs of others first. A servant leader, rather than amass power, helps others develop their true talents. We watch a series of short video clips from priests and lay leaders who discuss this theme and bring up biblical examples—the stories of Moses, Ruth, Mary, and Peter—to explain the concept more fully.

The assembly breaks up into smaller groups to think about how they can be better leaders and better servants in their day-to-day lives. They talk about the bad habits that can prevent them from living out the vision of servant leadership. "Exhaustion from my job," says one of the lawyers, sometimes means that he is not a good spouse, not good at keeping in touch with his friends. Another person worries that what gets sacrificed in a busy life is time to oneself, time to reflect on one's actions and thoughts. A young woman tells a story about how even though her father ran a large nonprofit, "He didn't bring the stress of his work home." She admires that deeply now.

They talk about how they can be their "best selves." What if your best self—when you are happiest and most spiritually fulfilled—comes out when you are teaching third grade? But what if that is not "feasible" financially? The people in this room have all made tremendous financial sacrifices during the years of their service work. While many friends were taking jobs as management consultants, they were making just enough to live on in some of the poorest areas of the country.

And as long as they put off marriage and family, they don't mind continuing to make financial sacrifices. But for those in the room who are just married or headed in that direction, they worry about making ends meet, especially if they want to send their own kids to Catholic schools.

They talk about how you can "find meaning and purpose in your job," whatever it may be. In some sense, the transition is not easy. When they did ACE, one young man says, "The sacrifice was more tangible. Now it is harder to figure out." He wonders how we can do a better job "serving the people close to us, being present for the people in my life."

One young woman worries that maybe she is not helping those in her own community enough. "Christ never left a forty-square mile area. We have all this technology and this ability to travel. It's a temptation to think bigger and do grander things." One can hear again here the young-adult impulse to go local.

Megan Adzima says these meetings "feel very focused and guided and the people are all on the same page, and that's a reassuring thing." They are a kind of "family" for her. While she is exploring different parishes and different Masses, she can participate in the Boston Advocates group and "feel a greater sense of mission." Over the course of our time there, the retreat's attendees grow noticeably closer. They talk about their teaching experiences, their personal lives, and their spiritual lives, even when they are outside of the formal group settings.

For dinner the monks of the abbey bring steaming pots of vegetable soup and warm homemade bread. There is no meat because it is a Friday during Lent. Through the course of the evening, students drink beer and wine and snack on trail mix and bulk-size bags of candy that they have brought themselves. It is easy to see the appeal of this relaxed setting.

The discussions, formal and informal, give young adults the opportunity to talk openly about their faith. For lay Catholics in this demographic group, there are not many settings where this occurs.

Some parishes have a reputation for attracting young adults. Mark Fennell, a lawyer who is married to one of the other participants, says that St. Cecilia's in downtown Boston "has an amazing liturgy and just leaves you filled." Mark and his wife, Liz, decided it was more important to try to build a community where they live in South Boston. But there is a downside. His parish, St. Bridget's, he notes, is a pretty "typical kind" of parish, where you "stay on to salute and go out. It's just very traditional." He says at St. Bridget's he feels like he is "part of the community, but not much more." That is, it's missing the spiritual fulfillment that a parish filled with young adults might provide. At these types of events run by the Boston Advocates, he says, "It's much easier to think and pray and just be quiet."

Father DelFra says it wasn't until ten years after they started ACE that they understood a real need for a "post program." He says that the church has been slow to give young laypeople more of a structure for their religious lives. "We are still working on those old assumptions that vocations will happen. It's hitting us that they're not happening. People are isolated, people are outside of the context of a practicing community."

A few years ago, Father DelFra tells me, the Notre Dame administration put out a small pamphlet for graduates directing them to parishes that had gained a reputation for engaging young people. The bishops, he said, objected. "They felt that it was taking more from the geographical parish." But Father DelFra seems to believe that young people will not simply go to their local parish because it is their local parish. If it is not lively or spiritually fulfilling enough for them, "I think they just stop going."

This is a contrast from Ray Cannata's view of the "theology of place." Geography used to be fundamental to a Catholic parish, but now many people are not concerned. Even young people who like the idea of living near the people they go to church with are frustrated by parishes that feel old and leadership that is tired. So they go elsewhere. Father DelFra tells me that young people "thrive on community," and if they're not getting it from their parish and their priest, they will simply leave it behind.

Rachel Grumley tells me that when she went home to visit her parents during college, she decided not to attend her geographical parish. This upset her father greatly, she recalls. "I chose to go not to our church but to one that was a lot farther away but had a large young adult population and great music and great homilies." When she came to live in Boston for her teaching stint, she remembers thinking she could "church shop. There are so many churches everywhere." In the "back of my mind," though, she always wondered, "Maybe I should go to the one based on where I live." But she couldn't do it. "I go to the one that fills me most," she tells me. She has to drive a ways to get there and "parking is sometimes a pain, but that's where I get the most and that's where I feel like I have a community."

What appeals to her in particular? "They have a phenomenal music ministry, and that is the first thing that people see and hear." It's why she kept coming back in the beginning. But she also says, "The homilies really apply to me. There is a life and an energy in the parish."

Here it seems the American Catholic Church is being faced with some strategic decisions about how to retain this younger generation. Should it be encouraging young Catholics to simply attend a select few parishes (mostly in major metropolitan areas) where they can find the sort of fulfilling music and spiritual messages that they're looking for? Or should it be looking for young people to be pioneers in lackluster parishes, hoping that they will take on more responsibility and turn the church into the kind of institution that other young people would like to attend? The answer needn't be one or the other, but right now it doesn't seem like the church has a well-thought-out plan with regard to this next generation.

But Grumley adds a couple of other key ideas that should signal to church leadership that young adults aren't simply looking to be served. Grumley tells me of the parish she found: "They have a really good focus on social justice and equality, on giving women an important role in the church. So I feel like I'm valued."

In this transition to more lay-run institutions, the Catholic Church will probably have to rely more on women. Since women in America, as we have noted, tend to be the ones who attend church more and who participate more in volunteer and service activities, the leadership will probably have to view the role of women differently.

This presents a serious challenge to the Catholic Church, whose reputation among American women has suffered significantly in recent years. Partly the church has been painted in an unfair light by liberal politicians who have suggested that its policies on contraception and abortion are part of an ongoing war on women. The images of the liberal Nuns on the Bus who have traveled the country speaking up in favor of the president's health-care program and against the Catholic Church's policies have not helped matters. But many women have also been deeply disturbed by the sexual abuse scandals, which leave them questioning an all-male priesthood. In fact, while more and more American churches and synagogues have put women in the pulpit, the Catholic Church (though its policy has not changed) seems like a throwback to another era.

According to a 2011 Pew survey of Americans, "Those who have left Catholicism outnumber those who have joined the Catholic Church by nearly a four-to-one margin. Overall, one-in-ten American adults (10.1 percent) have left the Catholic Church after having been raised Catholic." Of those who left, majorities of former Catholics who are now religiously unaffiliated cite dissatisfaction with Catholic teachings about abortion and homosexuality (56 percent), and almost half (48 percent) cite dissatisfaction with church teachings about birth control. Another 39 percent say they are unhappy with the church's treatment of women, and 33 percent say they don't like the church's teachings on marriage and divorce.

The church has made some changes in the past several years with regard to the participation of laywomen. The decline in vocations has meant that many parishes are relying more on laypeople, particularly on women in the pews. Women have started to hold leadership positions, even becoming "parish life directors," full-time executives who oversee administration, fund-raising, staffing, and strategic planning for parishes. They also do counseling, run services (though not Mass), and have other spiritual responsibilities, but they cannot offer the sacraments. Such changes, in part because they are somewhat controversial in the hierarchy, have not been widely publicized. If they were, though, one can imagine that young women might be willing to come back. These women want responsibility. They want to serve.

Most of my conversations with the folks at ACE come back to the idea of service as the most important vehicle for involving young people. Anthony Zavagnin had actually applied for a different kind of service when he was graduating from St. Anselm's College in New Hampshire. He wanted to join the military. He was rejected because he had asthma, but two days later he had an interview with ACE and it all "seemed to kind of fall into place." He liked the idea of the "discipline" that would have been required of him by the military and thought there was something similar that appealed to him in the idea of completely submersing himself in Catholic life for a couple of years.

Zavagnin grew up in a very traditional Catholic household— Italian on his father's side and Irish on his mother's. They went to church every week, but "faith was also cultural." His faith deepened a little in college, thanks to a religion course he took. But when he interviewed with ACE, he says, he was still "uncomfortable" when he was asked about a passage in the gospel. "I didn't know how I could express myself. It just wasn't something that we did growing up. When we'd go to Mass, we wouldn't sing. We were there but we were very private about things."

Being a Catholic school teacher, says Zavagnin, forced him to be "much more open about [faith]." He says, "I had to be willing to do that as part of my professional life, but it also kind of translated with my personal life, too." Becoming a teacher in a Catholic school—someone who was coming into a Catholic community to serve in a kind of leadership role—meant that he had to be willing to talk about faith with children and adults.

Now he holds hands with others during the reading of the

Our Father. He sings during Mass. He has done some readings in church as well.

For ACE teachers, though, their jobs often require them not only to be active participants in a Catholic community but also to represent the Catholic community to others. Pat Manning was placed in a Catholic school in Memphis after graduating from Notre Dame. The population at the school was about 90 percent Baptist, he tells me. (Especially in poorer urban areas, Catholic schools often serve a large number of non-Catholic students.)

"Not only were my students not Catholic," says Manning, "but I found many of them were not particularly engaged with their own traditions." He taught religion to his class, saying, "I was engaged in conversations of a spiritual nature on a daily basis. I tried to foster a habit of prayer in the classroom." He also helped the middle school students organize a spiritual retreat.

This habit of talking to his students about faith on a daily basis seems to have had the effect of strengthening his own faith. But other aspects of the program helped to ease Mannings path from college into participation in a regular religious community. For one thing, he went church shopping with his housemates. While many young people can find themselves at sea looking for a church on their own, going with a group makes the search somewhat less awkward.

Manning says he and his roommates were looking for a church with "decent preaching and hopefully some decent music." But it didn't bother him that there weren't many other single young people at the church they found. He already had that kind of community with his housemates and fellow ACE participants.

He is now enrolled in a doctoral program in Catholic education at Boston College. He is very involved in a parish near where he lives in Brighton, Massachusetts, and even teaches a confirmation class there. He lives with two other guys who are very strong in their faith as well. "I would say it is a community of sorts. We're very like-minded in the sense that we're all committed to the

Catholic faith, so the community aspect is important to us. We make a point at least once a week to have a meal together and usually invite somebody else to join us."

Manning will be leaving this "community" soon. He is engaged to a woman who is also strong in her faith and is a youth minister at a different parish.

As young people put off marriage and live away from their families for a longer period of time without getting married, there is more time for a kind of religious aimlessness. It can be awkward to live on one's own in a new city with a new job and then try to find a suitable religious congregation. It can be exhausting at the end of the week to have to go out alone and meet new people.

But the ACE program and others like it help young adults find like-minded friends to live with. They practice the habits of their faith inside the home—sharing meals together, for instance. They can also go out together to find a larger religious community to join together. All of this helps to foster the formation of new families, too. More than 10 percent of ACE graduates actually marry each other. Some find each other while teaching, but others meet through the Advocates alumni network.

Manning comes to meetings of the Boston Advocates occasionally to seek out new people and find out what is going on in the world of Catholic education, but ACE has helped him to put down permanent roots in the community. He regularly attends a formal parish. ACE has served as a kind of bridge, helping him and his fellow participants to go from a college atmosphere where religious life is easy and convenient to an adult world in which religious community is something that needs to be sought out and fully embraced.

Father DelFra says that Notre Dame alumni frequently come back to ask him about how to feel more connected to their faith now that they've graduated and are living on their own. He advises them to find a parish first, but if they're not up for that, they should try to find a spiritual counselor of some sort—"a monk or a priest you could meet with once a month and develop a relationship . . . It's a way that you're just checking in." In the meantime, he recommends "keeping a journal of whatever spiritual questions keep coming up for you."

During the course of the retreat Father DelFra offers to meet with people individually to hear confession. There is an acknowledgment that even the people in this room may not yet have found a permanent religious home or a priest with whom they feel comfortable speaking.

Father DelFra and the other administrators of the ACE program want to find ways that young adults can get what they need out of Catholicism. However, he emphasizes to his charges that this is not enough. "You can't just be a spiritual consumer. You have to be a spiritual producer because other people need what you have." In fact, he says, that's one of the "mottoes" of ACE and the Advocates. Being a spiritual producer—that is, serving the community—doesn't end when your formal time of service is over. The Advocates do organize other service activities.

But being a spiritual producer also involves understanding the liturgy and helping to lead a parish. Father DelFra describes a book that ACE recently published, *Five Minutes with Christ*. The book contains a series of gospel reflections: "Each reflection is based on an event in the life of Jesus and invites the reader to connect with him in the chaos of daily life."

Father DelFra hopes that the teachers in the program and the graduates will take these reflections and "empower their understanding of the church." He wants them to go from "*What can it do for me?* to *I'm a part of the church; what can I do to go about this?*"

Though Liz Fenell, Mark's wife, had been going to church from a young age, she recognized that something was missing from her religious life when she began to attend Boston College. "The first Sunday I woke up and I remember thinking to myself, *Huh, I don't have to go to Mass. No one is waking me up to say, 'Let's go.'*" She went anyway, just "out of habit," she tells me.

But when she got there and looked at all of her classmates in the pews, she thought, *They have something that I don't have, but it's something that I want. To me, it seemed like they owned their faith, whereas I had just accepted a faith I was raised in.* Liz ended up with a minor in theology. A class she took on St. Ignatius had a particularly strong impact on her, especially the silent retreat in which the class culminated. "It was a time I can really pinpoint where I was able to recognize a companionship with Christ, that I was never alone."

One of the things that drew Liz to ACE was the spiritual component of the program. But she was still "nervous" about losing the connection with her faith that she had gained in college. She worried about going from college religious life, in which "the homilies from the priest are so direct that you feel like they're talking to you," to a parish "where it's a lot harder. There are kids and adolescents and older people." It's not tailored to young adults.

Liz was sent to teach in Mississippi when she was accepted to ACE. She arrived just before Hurricane Katrina hit, and she found that the disaster brought the whole community together. Like the men and women at Redeemer in New Orleans, they have found that tragedy has a way of cementing a religious community. Several years later Liz is still connected with the people there. Twelve people from her community flew up to Rhode Island for her wedding. She and her husband have flown down there so that they could introduce their friends to their son, Patrick.

Liz has talked to a lot of her peers, graduates of other Catholic colleges, and found that they had fallen away from their faith, especially "if they didn't do some sort of service program and they went right into the corporate world or into some other graduate school that might not be faith-based."

Some of them do come back when they start to get married and have families of their own, but even then, someone has to take the initiative and invite people in. Liz has become a lector at St. Bridget's and likes to tell the people in her "moms' group" that they should come check out her parish. "If you're interested in bringing your family to church, know that we're always in the back row at 10:30 Mass. Anyone is more than welcome to join us."

Liz and Mark have gone out of their way to try to bring more young adults and more young families into their parish. Mark acknowledges that the parish can be seen as the kind of church where "all the old ladies run it and it's very structured and everyone just walks in and does their thing. They aren't really calling for volunteers." In other words, it's the kind of place where it would be easy to be a spiritual consumer.

But the kind of service that Liz did in ACE and that Mark did in the Jesuit Volunteer Corps have prepared them to take a much more active role. As Mark tells me, "I do think you need to put some responsibilities on the twenty- and thirty-somethings." He says that young adults "have to reach out and meet people and invite people to have lunch with you. No one is going to come up to you in a Catholic church necessarily and say, 'Would you like to redesign our young adult program?'" Mark thinks too many people in his generation are "waiting around for that." Young laypeople must start to take a more active role. He says, "Priests are hurting. They're just so overstretched."

His experience has been that, when he has offered, people have welcomed the help. Liz and a friend of hers have organized to have coffee and donuts after Mass so that the community has an opportunity for more socializing. The pastor told them, "Please, open the doors. Tell people to come in."

The ACE program and others like it are still relatively small. It is not easy to get young people just out of college (many of them with significant debt) to commit to a year, let alone two, of a low-paying job even if it is a meaningful one. Of course, ACE doesn't need hundreds of thousands of participants in order to make a difference in the way the Catholic Church appeals to young adults. It only needs to train leaders.

Father DelFra's view of the ACE alumni as a kind of lay order is strategic. If a few men and women who have done ACE or the Jesuit Volunteer Corps can make their way into some of the more lackluster parishes across the country and turn them into the kind of vibrant places—communities with good music and spiritual leadership, strong friendships and extended families, all with opportunities to serve—that young adults want to go, they will have returned the Catholic Church to the center of spiritual life it had been for generations.

4

What's NEXT?

*Channeling the Enthusiasm of Birthright Israel
into a Permanent Jewish Commitment*

AT 8 P.M. on a Thursday night in the fall of 2012, the music was
pumping and the lights were flashing but hardly anyone was
dancing at a club on the West Side of Manhattan. Instead, the
hundred or so patrons in their twenties and thirties were crowded
around the two open bars, embracing old friends and joking about
the dance-floor games that were coming later—the limbo, freeze
dance, and so on. If the games and the empty dance floor weren't
enough of a tipoff, perhaps the bunches of balloons tied all over
the room were. This was supposed to be a bar mitzvah, but one for
an organization, not a boy on the cusp of becoming a young man.

The celebration was for the thirteenth year of a program called
Taglit-Birthright Israel. (*Taglit* is Hebrew for discovery.) And the
three-hundred-plus people who eventually arrived for the combination reunion and fund-raiser were mostly alumni—Jews who
had received from the program a free ten-day trip to Israel before
they turned age twenty-six.

Established by Jewish philanthropists Charles Bronfman and
Michael Steinhardt, among others, in collaboration with the
Israeli government and various Jewish communal organizations,
Birthright's goal is "to strengthen Jewish identity, Jewish commu-
nities, and solidarity with Israel." As the generation that experi-
enced the Holocaust and the creation of Israel grew older and

died, younger Jews began to view the issue of a Jewish state with less and less urgency.

Birthright's founders wanted to counter the waning interest in Judaism among the young. So far, the organization has sent more than three hundred thousand Jews from fifty-nine countries to Israel—mostly from the United States and Canada.

Mark Shapiro, a former consultant for McKinsey & Co. who worked on the original plans for Birthright, says that some of the impetus for the project came from the 1990 Jewish Population Survey that showed an intermarriage rate for American Jews of greater than 50 percent. The children, and especially the grandchildren, of these unions showed declining interest in Judaism. "The idea was to give everybody some connection to their heritage," Shapiro says.

In the years since the Birthright program was launched, Leonard Saxe, the director of the Cohen Center for Modern Jewish Studies at Brandeis University, has led a research group studying its effects, and he has been impressed. "In the modern world," Saxe says, "we all have multiple identities, from where we were born to who our parents are. The Birthright trip has put Jewish identity closer to the top of that list."

Saxe's team has found, for instance, that Birthright produced a small increase in the likelihood that young Jews will light candles or have a special meal on Shabbat. Among participants, 51 percent reported lighting candles at least sometimes, compared with 42 percent among nonparticipants.

Jenna Garson, who attended the bar mitzvah event and went on the trip in 2008, says that Birthright didn't change her Jewish practice very much. She still doesn't go to synagogue much beyond the High Holidays. What really changed, she says, was her attachment to Israel.

It is a common result of the Birthright trips: In a 2008 survey, 55 percent of participants felt that Israel is a "source of pride," compared with 35 percent of nonparticipants. Forty percent felt that the Jewish state is a "refuge for persecuted Jews," compared with 22 percent of nonparticipants.

Brian Smith went on the trip in September 2007 and said the "most moving part of the experience" was a visit to Masada, where in the first century Romans laid siege to a fortress held by Jewish rebels, who chose to die rather than succumb. Smith says he was brought up with a strong sense of his Jewish roots, which later weakened while he was an undergraduate at Indiana University. The Birthright trip sparked a stronger sense of identity, he says, and inspired him to "put my best foot forward to further a culture that has been around for fifty-seven hundred years."

In this sense, the Birthright program has been wildly successful. The cohort eligible for the trip is about one hundred thousand each year. About a third of those go. According to organizers, the aim is to get that number to more than half in the next few years. It is hard to imagine another program that would touch the lives of such a large percentage of coreligionists.

Sending such a significant portion of the young Jewish population on a ten-day trip to Israel has not only given recipients a strong connection to that country and to the culture. It has also energized them, giving them a certain kind of excitement about what they may have previously thought of as an old-fashioned or even dying faith.

But Jewish leaders now also face the challenge of trying to funnel the excitement that comes from a Birthright trip into a more permanent Jewish experience. They are not the first community to struggle with this question. The kind of feeling that young people gain from a Birthright trip is very similar, it seems to me, to the emotion that comes when young Christians embark on short-term missionary experiences. Whether they are building homes in Mexico or wells in Africa, these trips put young people into close contact with their fellow faithful, providing an intense experience in a location far from home. Many young people describe going on such trips during college or just after as overwhelming and eye-opening.

Unfortunately, there is often no obvious way to translate that experience into their day-to-day lives.

Writing in the *Wall Street Journal* in 2008, Evan Sparks described some of the research about the effects of short-term Christian missions. "Calvin College sociologist Kurt Ver Beek surveyed U.S. missionaries who built homes in Honduras after Hurricane Mitch in 1998. After coming down from a post-trip 'high,' the short-termers did not evince much change in their lives. Only 16 percent reported 'significant positive impact,' including in prayer, friendships and financial giving."

So what will give the Birthright experience staying power? Michael Steinhardt is actually a self-described atheist. He wants to further the Jewish people and Jewish culture, not necessarily the Jewish religion. Disentangling these three elements is hard, needless to say, and many Jewish leaders would say that they shouldn't be. But it does seem that Birthright is succeeding on Steinhardt's terms. According to Saxe's most recent study, released in 2012, "Among married non-Orthodox respondents, Taglit participants are 45 percent more likely than non-participants to be married to a Jew."

David Manchester went on a Birthright trip his sophomore year in college. He was already very interested in foreign policy, particularly in the Middle East, but he said he wanted to have a "personal narrative of experiencing Israel." When he returned he became more focused on the "pro-Israel movement in America" and got more involved with his campus Hillel organization as well. He recently helped lead a Birthright trip. David describes an exercise I heard about from a number of Birthright alumni. "We asked people to go to one of the four corners of the room depending on their level of agreement with the statement, 'I will only marry a Jew.'" He says that being in Israel "brings you back to the hierarchy of needs. We all have shelter and food. What are the next things? I really need to find someone I'm going to spend the rest of my life with."

According to organizers, a discussion of interfaith marriage is not a required part of the program, but Birthright contracts with different providers, and many of those decide to include it.

When I interview the men and women at the bar mitzvah celebration, I am told by many of the rumor that Steinhardt himself will pay for your wedding (some have it as "your honeymoon") if you marry someone you met on your Birthright trip. Many of the people I interviewed described meeting their spouse or at least a significant other on a trip (and plenty of others meet through mutual friends who went on a trip). It is easy to see why the trip's environment would fuel romantic relationships.

A number of young adults describe the Birthright experience to me as a kind of alternative spring break trip. A group of college kids—some of whom know each other, some of whom don't—are brought to a foreign country (where the drinking age is eighteen). They live in close quarters and are taken to beautiful places. They are led in discussions about personal issues from spiritual beliefs to politics to marriage.

Marrying another Jew may make someone more likely to do Jewish things—most importantly, perhaps, raising children Jewish. But will those children feel any particular connection to Judaism? Will they see anything worthy in the faith or the culture? Or will they, too, have to be offered a trip to Israel in order to make a commitment to their people?

A few years ago, organizers started to think more seriously about how the program's alumni could translate their experiences into greater participation in the Jewish community and a greater substantive understanding of Jewish traditions and beliefs. Birthright NEXT was formed to encourage the process. According to Morlie Levin, the organization's CEO, this generation of Jews may have a "deeper knowledge about Judaism, rituals, and cultural matters than their parents' generation." She cites the increase in attendance at Jewish day schools and the spike in travel to Israel. On the other hand, "They're not involved in the institutions that previous generations developed." This leaves NEXT with two alternatives—either try to push young Jewish adults into those institutions or get them to form new ways of connecting with Judaism. NEXT is trying to do a little of both.

Russell Gottschalk is the product of a mixed marriage himself and grew up without very strong religious leanings. He attended Sunday school but never had a bar mitzvah and tells me that growing up in Atlanta, "Judaism was not really a source of pride." That changed when he attended Emory University, whose population is almost a third Jewish. He went on a Birthright trip while he was in school. His most "impactful experiences," he tells me, were at the Dead Sea and climbing Mount Masada. He also was fascinated by Independence Hall in Tel Aviv. Even the "natural wonders of the country" made an impact. "It was a magical experience for me." He liked being with Jews of all different backgrounds and coming to "pray together."

Some people found a connection to God on the trip, says Gottschalk. But "I relate to Judaism through humanity. It's through interpersonal connections. There was such energy coming from people at the Western Wall, even though most of us didn't know each other." When Gottschalk returned from Birthright he says he was "energized personally and professionally." He interned with the Atlanta Jewish Film Festival. Later he founded the Atlanta Jewish Music Festival. Since graduating from college, he has become more active in the Atlanta Jewish community, organizing activities for young professionals.

Gottschalk is actually among the more religiously observant Birthright alumni I interviewed. He does not work on Saturday or answer his cell phone. He wears a yarmulke when he is studying or praying. He observes the High Holidays and goes to synagogue almost every week, but he is not a member. "I think that institutions are automatically starting at a disadvantage by being institutions." His generation isn't even into gym memberships, he tells me. Why would they want to buy a ticket for the services offered by a synagogue?

But there seems to be a bigger problem for people like Gottschalk. He reiterates the point that Saxe has made about this generation having multiple identities. "If I were going to describe myself, I wouldn't use Jewish in the top five descriptors. I'm from Atlanta, an artist, I love to play Frisbee. Judaism is a big part of my identity but not the main label." Jewish leaders might see this as a sign of trouble if someone like Gottschalk prioritizes his Frisbee playing ahead of his Judaism. It suggests that maybe trying to get young adults to engage with religious communities without engaging with the institutions in those communities might be problematic.

But NEXT is trying to make Judaism less intimidating for young people. One way to do that is by taking rituals and learning out of the synagogue and into the homes of friends.

Among the biggest NEXT initiatives are Shabbat dinners hosted by Birthright participants. Over fifteen thousand such meals have been held. Levin refers to these as "peer-to-peer" activities because—aside from sending a box that has some candles and music—NEXT mostly leaves it up to the Shabbat hosts to organize the evening. They can invite their friends—both Jewish and non-Jewish. Emily Comisar, who helps run the program, tells me that "many of the hosts are excited to share their rituals and traditions with their non-Jewish friends. It's sort of an issue of pride to them, which is actually very cool." The hosts can serve kosher food or not. They can cook or order in. They can discuss Jewish matters over the course of the evening or the religious content can be restricted to simply saying the blessings over the challah, the candles, and the wine.

Many of the most important rituals of Judaism are based in the home, so a big challenge for any organization trying to encourage a greater commitment to Jewish life is getting people to incorporate Jewish practices inside the confines of their home rather than just getting them to attend an event at a synagogue or Jewish Community Center. By giving hosts this responsibility of organizing the dinner, NEXT is not only empowering them to lead Jewish rituals but it is also ensuring that these activities are brought into their personal space.

Levin is reluctant to say that the goal of NEXT is simply to raise the number of people doing Jewish things. But as she tells me about the number of people who have celebrated Shabbat through a NEXT program (200,000) or the number of hosts who have sponsored them (over 8,200), I am reminded a little bit of Chabad. An orthodox Jewish sect, Chabad doesn't seem to have much in common with this crowd but Chabad emissaries wander the streets of New York and other cities trying to get Jews to participate in discrete mitzvot—lighting the Chanukah candles, laying tefillin, etc.—and each act they believe brings us all closer to the coming of the Messiah.

What does each Shabbat observance bring us closer to in the eyes of NEXT? It's not entirely clear, but it is true that many of the people who participate in these dinners would not otherwise have had any noticeable connection to Judaism that day or that week or that month.

Levin says that NEXT is trying to "create more transparency in the home community so that Birthrighters can find opportunities for Jewish living and learning." She says that the current generation of young adults "will not be a pipeline of folks marching in lockstep to fill the ranks of volunteers or donors or professionals with all of the existing communities." Rather she sees that the "marketplace" will let some institutions survive while others will not. She wonders in particular about regional Jewish federations—collections of social service agencies that raise and distribute money in Jewish communities across the country. "They are going to start struggling to make sure they have a mission and purpose that finds a way to make collectivity relevant in an age of individualism."

I meet Rachel Hodes, Maxie Kalish, and Shoshana Smolen at their apartment in the Murray Hill neighborhood of Manhattan. The three are recent college graduates and their apartment is a "Moishe House," one of dozens of homes across the world that are supposed to serve as "hubs" of Judaism, particularly for those between the ages of twenty-one and thirty-two. In return for a large rent subsidy, the residents of the house (who can live here for up to four years) agree to provide a certain number of Jewish activities, holiday celebrations, service projects and educational opportunities for the community. Sometimes they host NEXT Shabbat dinners, as they are this evening.

When I arrive, the three are moving around furniture and arranging the trays of takeout kosher Mexican food in the small galley kitchen and cramped living room. Beside the candles and the Kiddush cup and the challah, the women have set up a laptop on the table to record the occasion on the NEXT website.

Hodes and Kalish both grew up in Reformed Jewish households and went on Birthright trips. Smolen grew up in a more Conservative home and was not eligible for Birthright because she had been on another organized trip to Israel as a teenager. All three were engaged in Jewish life in college. Smolen and Hodes went to Rutgers University and Kalish attended Clark University in Massachusetts. But when they moved to New York, none of them really found any Jewish institutions to affiliate with.

"It's not my number one priority," says Kalish, though "if I found one I really clicked with and liked I would go." Smolen, who went to Jewish day schools and Jewish camp growing up, says that "Jewish life sort of fell by the wayside" after college. She moved home before she started law school and would sometimes have Shabbat dinner with her family, but between the stresses of school and trying to maintain a connection with the law school community even though she was a commuter, Jewish practice wasn't a priority. She had a couple of close Jewish friends who lived near her family, but "many of my other Jewish connections had moved to other cities. The peer group that I had participated in Jewish life with wasn't there as much."

This theme came up again and again in my interviews with young adults of all religious stripes—when a group of friends who are coreligionists starts to dissipate, the religious observance starts to fall off. Practicing a faith does not, on its surface, seem like a team sport. There's no reason you can't go to synagogue or church alone. But people don't.

Moishe House has provided a kind of alternative Jewish institution for its residents. While all three tell me that they are in no hurry to join a synagogue, particularly because of the dues they would have to pay, they are happy to take an active role in Jewish life by inviting friends and strangers into their home to celebrate Jewish holidays and organize religious rituals and service projects.

During the course of the evening, about two dozen people arrive. Many have brought along school supplies to donate to kids living in the path of Hurricane Sandy. Some are friends of the girls, others are friends of friends, and others are strangers who have moved to the area recently and are interested in connecting with Jewish life.

Some of the men are wearing yarmulkes, and one offers to say the blessing over the wine. The attendees' knowledge about Judaism ranges from next to nothing to that of a young woman named Dina who grew up Orthodox and spent time studying in Israel. She left her ritual observances behind after college, but Birthright brought her back—at least part way.

"Religiosity," she tells me, "doesn't matter on Birthright." She says the trip "opened my eyes to other Jewish young adults" from a variety of backgrounds. She appreciates the atmosphere of these events, that there is "not judgment. It's nice to be able to be myself."

Another woman at the event, Aimee Weiss, tells me that she thinks that she is "living through a Jewish framework." She doesn't place much emphasis on "religious obligations." But she thinks that "Jewish culture and values are beautiful." She is single now, and she is not sure that she will ever join a synagogue even when she gets married and has children. "In their current incarnation they are too denominational. I don't see myself in that framework." She does not identify with any particular Jewish denomination. "I would check off the 'Just Jewish' box."

The organizers call the event to order and Smolen asks if anyone wants to light the candles. "It can be a dude," she jokes. (Traditionally, candle lighting is a role reserved for women.) "We're totally egal," she says, using the shorthand for egalitarian. After someone recites the Kiddush, the socializing begins, and by the time I leave around 10 p.m., it is hard to carry on a conversation over the raucous laughter in the apartment.

If millennials tend to coalesce into urban tribes now, eschewing institutions and simply wandering as groups of friends, then this peer-to-peer kind of activity seems to have a good chance of success. NEXT covers the cost of the food for these events—offering between ten and fifteen dollars per person for the event.

It is not as if the hosts are doing this so they can throw lavish dinner parties for their friends, but some Jewish leaders worry about the precedent that Birthright and NEXT are setting for young Jews by taking care of all these expenses.

David Bryfman, director of the New Center for Collaborative Leadership at the Jewish Education Project, gave a talk in 2012 called "The Consequences of Free," in which he suggested that Jewish organizations stop covering the cost of Jewish experiences for young people:

> So congratulations to all of you out there who have managed to get large numbers on your free programs. All you've managed to do is prove the point that people will do absolutely anything for free. And the numbers are staggering. But now ask yourselves, why would any-

one who has been thrown free Jewish life milestones now think they are valuable enough to pay for others of more or greater significance? . . . Are we as a community brave enough to hit "pause" if not "reset"? Can we take a step back and look at the consequences of free and see if we can utilize its undoubted power, its magnitude, to really transform the Jewish community as a whole?

Bryfman is probably right that giving away trips and dinners may devalue them in the eyes of recipients. A few Birthright participants mentioned in interviews having misgivings that the trip to Israel was free. They hoped alums would give at least a small donation to the organization as a way of showing their gratitude for the gift.

Gary Rosenblatt, the editor of *Jewish Week*, wrote that the program may give young Jews the impression that participation in Jewish life has no costs: "Surely free offers have appeal for the targeted audience, but is this a sign of strategic planning or desperation?"

It is probably a little bit of both.

Synagogue dues can certainly create a kind of sticker shock for young adults. Well over a thousand dollars in some metropolitan areas, such membership costs do not sit well with a generation deep in student loan debt and without many good job prospects. Unlike Protestant and Catholic churches, which ask for unspecified contributions each week, or the Mormon Church, which asks for a certain percentage of income each month (and trains its young people to give this from the time they are eight years old), synagogues just present members with a large annual bill.

In response, some have started offering lower prices for younger members, but the expectations haven't changed much. The unwillingness or inability of young people to pay for institutional membership is not likely to go away soon. But there is certainly something to be said for managing expectations. Parents must talk more to young people growing up about why and to what extent they give to Jewish institutions, training them to donate from allowances or summer jobs, and young adults must be made to understand "the consequences of free."

In the meantime, it may be useful to think of ways to put the service ethic of this generation to the test. Would they be willing to offer some sort of work to the community in lieu of paying dues? Not only would this allow congregations and their younger members a kind of fair trade, but it would presumably make young adults invest the kind of time in the community that would make them more likely to value membership later in life.

NEXT has not entirely given up on the idea that young people might someday become a part, even paying members, of already existing institutions. But young adult Jews are in a kind of transition period where they need something more fun and exciting, something more like what Hillel provided them in college. Perhaps they need a weekly gathering where they can see plenty of people their own age and participate in more exciting services.

With a half an inch of snow on the ground on a Friday night in January 2013, it felt like Washington, DC, was shutting down for the weekend. The Metro seemed empty at rush hour, but there were more than three hundred people, mostly young adults, streaming into Adas Israel, a Conservative synagogue in the Cleveland Park neighborhood. Many of them were there to "Shabbat Hop." The local Jewish Federation combines forces with NEXT DC to get young adults to try out a new synagogue each month.

The word "hopping" does not generally bring smiles to the faces of religious leaders. They have heard the testimony of experts on how Generation Y fears commitment, how its members don't like institutions, how they prefer to simply act like a roving "urban tribe," texting their whereabouts as they go. Faced with too many choices and paralyzed by the possibility of regret, they RSVP "maybe" to every Evite. For a generation like this, in other words, "hopping" from one house of worship to the next is just about the last thing most religious leaders want to encourage.

But inside Adas there is warmth. The hundreds of chairs are arranged in a circle around one of the cantors and two other musicians as they offer a lively and moving evening service. For an hour and a half, people sway, clap, and sing. The Shabbat Hoppers are clustered on one side of the room. They embrace friends who come in late and do some chatting, but it doesn't appear to distract them from the calming service at the end of a long week. They stay for a buffet-style dinner afterward and continue to linger until close to 10 p.m. A number of people tell me they will go out afterward for drinks.

Jenna Lowy, a twenty-seven-year-old fund-raiser who has been living in Washington for five years, says that her "hesitation in going to services before has been not knowing anyone." But coming with a group has made it easier. Becky Porter, the cochair of Shabbat Hopping this year, tells me that her boyfriend lived next door to a synagogue in Bethesda, Maryland, but whenever he would go, "No one would approach him to welcome him." So he started to Shabbat Hop.

He is not alone. A 2012 article in *Jewish Week* complained about the "customer service" problem in the Jewish community. "We walk into synagogues and schools and JCCs, and no one says hello. Few know our names (maybe for months or years). A friend in an interfaith marriage says that when he takes his wife to shul, no one talks to them. When he goes to his wife's church, everyone comes over to greet them."

David Polonsky, director of communications at Adas, tells me that when he moved to Washington a few years ago and called around to find out about High Holiday services, he was told they would cost him hundreds of dollars. "I'm a young person calling them and asking them for a Jewish experience," but no one even asked for his name, let alone told him to come try out the synagogue. Shabbat Hopping at least makes people feel welcome.

Adas Israel, the Washington Hebrew Congregation (a Reform temple), and the Sixth and I synagogue (a nondenominational one) have all made a big deal of welcoming young professionals— even when there is no Shabbat Hopping event. Sixth and I offers a different kind of service every week. Other synagogues bring in music and offer Shabbat meals, even open bars.

Still, even when synagogues are welcoming, few young people seem to have an interest in joining in any official capacity. Of the dozen or so people I interviewed at Adas, no one has any plans to put down permanent roots, financially or spiritually, in a synagogue any time soon. Stacy Miller, a twenty-nine-year-old teacher, tells me that she has set up a social group for Jewish young professionals in northern Virginia. She will join a synagogue "some day," she tells me. "Right now, I get to go to different places and meet new people."

Sixth and I has a "nonmembership model," according to Beth Semel, who works on programming there. Almost all of the synagogue's activities are specifically geared toward young adults, and she says that the leadership doesn't worry about young people jumping around from one place to another.

"This just goes with the territory," Rabbi Aaron Miller of the Washington Hebrew Congregation says. "The twenty- and thirty-something crowd in DC is just very transient." His synagogue even sponsors Metro Minyan, which rents out space in local churches near Metro stops for a Shabbat service and dinner. By having it in a different place every week, it's "neutral territory." It's harder for young people to feel intimidated, he tells me, when everyone is new to the space.

Shabbat Hopping was launched in 2007 by Rachel Gerrol. The product of a Jewish father "who didn't really care about Judaism" and a mother who was herself the daughter of two Christian ministers, Gerrol didn't have much interest in or knowledge of Judaism until she went on a Birthright trip in college.

When she returned, she found that her college Hillel did not really have much to offer for someone who knew nothing about Judaism. And it was worse than that. She recalls being twenty years old and going to her first Rosh Hashanah service. "It was the first year I'd be a Jew." She says when she got there, there was a book on her seat. When she went to church, it was traditional to place the hymnal on the floor under the seat until it was time in the service to use it. She put the Jewish prayerbook on the floor, and several women came over to scold her and told her to kiss it. This is the traditional response if a siddur (Jewish prayerbook) is accidentally dropped or even if it is temporarily put down. It is considered a holy object.

But Gerrol didn't know and no one offered to explain. So she took a few years off from synagogue. When she decided she wanted to go back, she says, she didn't want to go alone. She wanted a service that would be done in an "explanatory manner." And she wanted the other congregants to know "that there are people who don't know." She didn't want to go into a sanctuary and have to hear people saying, "Who's that girl who doesn't know where to put her book?" or "Who's that Asian guy?"

Eighty-five people showed up to the first Shabbat Hopping event. Gerrol describes a "sense of fellowship of people who were interested to explore and study together." It was followed by a dinner in which people were singing songs, and if they didn't know the words, they were "banging on the table." Two years later, they began to have lay-led services where two hundred people were showing up.

Gerrol says there is "beauty to what institutions can provide." "First of all it is a roof, and second of all it is a community. I didn't know any Jews." She said the key to the success of Shabbat Hopping was making a "safe space where people know they wouldn't be the outsider."

And Gerrol has seen a progression. Some of the young adults have continued to Shabbat Hop, but others have moved out to the suburbs, had kids, and joined a multigenerational synagogue.

While she is sorry that Shabbat Hopping has moved away from some of its "explanatory" role, she sees that a lot of good has come of it. "Interfaith couples," in particular, she says, "have embraced a type of Jewish learning and life. And many non-Jewish partners have experienced that for the first time."

According to a survey conducted by the Synagogue 3000 Studies Institute, only 25 percent of Jews under the age of thirty-five belong to a synagogue—compared with 37 percent for Jews ages forty-five to fifty-four. But for unmarried Jews under the age of forty-five, that number is only 19 percent. For some, this may mean that they are between religious institutions. But others may be skipping out on faith entirely.

As one young adult told Hannah Seligson, the author of *Mission Adulthood*, "What people in the past may have gotten from church, I get from the Internet and Facebook. That is our religion." So maybe Shabbat Hopping is the best that religious leaders can hope for with this generation. Giving young adults regular exposure to *some* Jewish experience is certainly better than the alternative. Birthright has provided the Jewish community with a great launching point for young adults, but it is up to the institutional leaders to build on that and ensure that when participants return from their trips to Israel, they can see the next steps in their Jewish journey—preferably from the tarmac.

5

A Ward of Their Own

*How the Mormon Church Is Turning Twenty-Somethings
into Community Leaders*

CORY DUCKWORTH was twenty-one when he married his high school sweetheart. They had been dating since the age of sixteen. Duckworth, who is now the bishop of a Mormon ward in American Fork, Utah (not far from Salt Lake City), says his story was not all that uncommon back then, thirty-odd years ago. His son Cameron, however, is twenty-four and not dating anyone, let alone married.

Cameron is finishing his degree at Utah Valley University—he took two years off to go on a mission. He tells me that he does feel some pressure to find a wife. "I mean, I'm not old, but you definitely get people who are like, 'Oh yeah, marriage is great.' But then there are always the people who are like, 'Don't rush it.'" Cameron's father would prefer he speed things up a little, but he recognizes that something about this generation makes it somehow less ready for the responsibilities of adulthood, including marriage.

Bishop Duckworth, who also works as the vice president of student affairs at Utah Valley University, says that the "whole idea of delayed adolescence is very much real. You have people in their twenties who are still playing video games and, you know, engaging in activities that aren't particularly productive." Moreover, he sees the phenomenon of helicopter parenting as contributing to the infantilization of young adults. When the elder Duckworth left for college, he says, "The last thing I ever would have dreamed of was taking my mom to college to help me get registered. And yet where I work, I see parents in our hallways all the time . . . and we get calls from them when something doesn't go right." Duckworth says he sees "a shift over time in terms of the level of responsibility and connectedness to the world" that young adults display.

Today, the average age of marriage among members of the Church of Jesus Christ of Latter-day Saints is on the rise, which is creating some profound challenges for the leaders of the faith in terms of their ability to keep young adults active Mormons. According to the 2006 General Social Survey (the last time researchers asked the question about age at first marriage), Mormons married at 22.6. If we look at the whole decade of the 1990s, Mormons were at 21.6. In a survey I conducted in 2010, it was up to 23. This age may not seem high yet, but if the Mormon population follows the trend of the rest of the American population (albeit at a slower pace), the church could be in real trouble.[5]

The focus on marriage in the Mormon Church is a major reason for the faith's intense growth over the past few decades. Members marry younger than their secular and other religious counterparts and have a higher-than-average number of children. The church offers both theological and practical support for these families. Latter-day Saints (LDS) members believe they can live on with their spouse and children after they die. In this life, they are encouraged to spend a lot of time together. Once a week, there is even a church-mandated "family home night," in which members are asked to stay at home with their spouse and children, learning Scriptures, eating together, and playing games.

All of this emphasis on marriage and family pushes young people to put down roots early and get themselves and their children involved in church life. But as young Mormons start to follow the pattern of other Americans their age and put off marriage, the years after they leave their parents' home can become a time for religious wandering.

Single young adults are much harder to pin down. A number of years ago, the Mormon Church organized wards that are specifically for singles between the ages of eighteen and thirty. Members in this age group were encouraged to go to a different worship service from their parents or younger siblings. These singles wards would still have an older (married) person at their head, but all of the other congregational leadership roles would be held by single men and women in this age group.

This model of purposefully segregating young adults from other demographic groups is not a common one for churches. Some churches end up attracting a specific age group, but rarely is it by design. Other churches may hold separate services for children or teens, but they don't limit the attendance of adults by age group.

The LDS Church has found this model to be a success—so much so that, in 2011, church leadership doubled down on these wards. They eliminated the distinction between so-called student wards and Young Single Adult wards (YSAs) to make sure that young adults had more opportunities to meet potential mates whether they were enrolled in a university or not and to clarify where a young person in this age group should be attending services. This seemingly small alteration in church policy affected hundreds of thousands of young adults in Utah alone.

Before this shift, it was easy for a young person who was, say, attending Brigham Young University (BYU) to go to a student ward during the school year. But upon coming home, that person would have to pick a new ward—a local student ward, a family ward, or a YSA ward. Many people ended up drifting from one to another or simply falling through the cracks. The church was having trouble keeping track of attendance, not to mention tithing.

More and more the church leaders are trying to make the YSA

ward the default place where young people go when they turn eighteen, rather than just offering them the option to attend. The bishops go visit the family wards and talk to the students finishing high school to encourage them to join a YSA after graduation.

"This age group tends to drift a little bit, to different units, different wards," said Elder Steven E. Snow of the Presidency of the Seventy, on the announcement of this change. "We hope it will provide enhanced opportunities for them to serve in leadership positions, and to teach, to lead . . . We hope it enhances their opportunities to meet other people and to do meaningful service, and we want to deliver these opportunities in their geographic area."

In other words, the biggest challenges of engaging young adults, according to many church leaders, are young adults' tendencies to prolong adolescence and shirk responsibility and their decision to delay marriage and put down roots in a community. In response, the LDS Church has decided to expand the opportunities for this generation to lead and to meet others in the same age group.

Tatiana Boyle graduated from high school a little over a year ago. She says she had to decide whether to continue to attend her family's ward or come to the YSA ward in American Fork, Utah. "I thought I'd feel more comfortable with my family ward," she says. But after a few visits she says she felt like a "super-senior, you know, the kid who goes back to their high school for all the games. I felt like everyone was looking at me and wondering, 'What are you still doing here?'"

Jessica Paulson is almost twenty-four years old and has been a member of the American Fork YSA ward since she graduated from high school. She has held a variety of positions, including Relief Society president, which is the head of the women's arm of the ward. (The official mission of the Relief Society is to "prepare women for the blessings of eternal life by helping them increase their faith and personal righteousness, strengthen families and homes, and help those in need.") Of the YSA ward, she says, "I feel like it's a place where I can grow in my own personal convictions and have an opportunity to lead, to teach more than I would if I were in a ward with older adults."

This idea that many more leadership opportunities are available to Mormons in these YSAs is emphasized again and again during my interviews. Taylor Jones, a twenty-one-year-old who recently returned from his mission, is serving as the financial clerk for the ward. "It's a really good experience. A lot of the callings that older people would get, we have instead. It gives us a lot of experience."

YSAs have also served an especially important role for returning missionaries. These young men often have a difficult transition when they return home after two years out in the field, proselytizing and working for the church long hours every day.

"A lot of them were so geared toward their mission," says Bishop Duckworth, "that they never bothered to think about what happens after that." He has seen more than a few of these young men fall away from the church when they return home. "We try to get them here [at the YSA ward] as quickly as we can, give them a calling in the ward so that they can have a responsibility and something they're invested in." He encourages them to share their experiences with others in the ward. But it is a tough hurdle. "I try to convince them that the [soul-]saving practices they have been engaging in are just as important and valuable for the people who live right here as they were in South Africa."

Returning missionaries may find it difficult to transition from having a lot of responsibility in the church to holding a position that only requires a few hours a week of their time. (This is similar to the complaint one hears from ACE volunteers who say that their sacrifice during the program was "more tangible," but now it's "harder to figure out.") For most people, though, the YSA ward provides them with their first real experience with adult responsibilities—at least in the church. And the several hours a week they spend teaching Sunday school or working on the ward's finances or organizing services for needy members of the community provide them with a clear sense of purpose in lives that can seem otherwise tumultuous.

Many of the people I interviewed did find it strange at first to see their peers in leadership roles. Boyle tells me she was surprised to see a guy she grew up with teaching religious education. "I remember when were in Sunday school together and he did not pay attention," she jokes. "It's funny, but at the same time I think it's just that we're all growing up."

Perhaps that realization is the one that the church leadership is looking for its young people to embrace. Even if you still think of yourself as a teenager, seeing your friends take on positions of responsibility or taking them on yourself helps you see yourself in a different, more mature light.

But what about marriage? Do these separate wards encourage young adults to meet, mingle, and find their matches? The responses seemed mixed. Many of the men and women I spoke with suggested that YSAs were better for them because there was *less* pressure to marry than would take place at the ward their parents attended.

While Paulson says she has never felt anything less than welcome at a family ward, "They do tend to focus a lot of their lessons on families and how to teach your children. When you are with people who are in your same situation in life," that is, people who are also single, "they can help you feel more like you belong." Jones tells me that the lessons are "geared toward us and what we're doing now."

All of this may encourage young men and women to be more active participants in their faith, but the dating landscape inside of a singles ward is still very fraught, according to most of the people I interviewed. For Boyle, the "weirdness" comes from the fact that she has known most of the people in the ward since she was young. "I can't see myself dating any of them." She says her brother did end up marrying someone in the ward, but many of the other young men and women feel as if the YSA ward is like a family.

So the extent that they can meet people at other wards through church activities helps their marriage prospects. But inside the ward, they feel it will be difficult if a relationship doesn't work out.

Chris Wermly, who recently returned from a mission in Guatemala, has been on a few dates with women in this ward. They haven't worked out, but, he says, "That doesn't keep me from coming back." Still, "It can be kind of awkward."

Bishop Duckworth complains that the people in his ward "don't even know how to date. They know how to hang out." One of the "sisters" (as Mormon women are called) in the ward told him that things have changed dramatically since he was young. "It used to be in the old days that people would date in order to find out if there was somebody they liked enough to marry. Today, no one will date you unless they're sure they want to marry you." Duckworth has concluded that people just aren't "diving in. And the older they get the more cautious they become." In this sense, it seems as though the dating culture of the outside world has started to infiltrate even the more insular Mormon communities in Utah.

Duckworth says he has been surprised at how much less concerned the young people in American Fork are about marriage than those at BYU. "We haven't got quite the same level of focus here," he tells me. One reason for that may simply be the wider American trends in marriage. As scholars like Kay Hymowitz and Charles Murray have noted, the upper classes in America are much more likely to marry and stay married than the lower classes. In his archetypal cities of Belmont and Fishtown (the former representing white-collar, educated suburbanites and the latter representing blue-collar high school graduates and dropouts), Murray describes the marriage divide in an article in the *Wall Street Journal*:

> In 1960, extremely high proportions of whites in both Belmont and Fishtown were married—94 percent in

Belmont and 84 percent in Fishtown. In the 1970s, those percentages declined about equally in both places. Then came the great divergence. In Belmont, marriage stabilized during the mid-1980s, standing at 83 percent in 2010. In Fishtown, however, marriage continued to slide; as of 2010, a minority (just 48 percent) were married. The gap in marriage between Belmont and Fishtown grew to 35 percentage points, from just 10.

As Hymowitz wrote in an article for *City Journal*, "The old-fashioned married-couple-with-children model is doing quite well among college-educated women. It is primarily among lower-income women with only a high school education that it is in poor health."

So marriage may prove to be more of a problem for religious institutions in lower-income working-class areas, like American Fork, which is also a reason for the institutions serving this population to redouble their efforts.

Those areas also face other challenges that are probably less common among BYU students. Cameron Duckworth says that he has seen friends drift away from church, in part because of drugs and alcohol. One friend tragically died of alcohol poisoning recently. His father, the bishop, says he regularly counsels young people with addiction issues, including Internet pornography. Even young people who are not facing these difficulties may struggle with their faith, of course. Cameron himself says there was a six-month period where he stopped coming to church. He says, "I knew I would always come back. It was just I had to figure out things for myself."

While college students have their own share of problems, the kids at BYU are generally on the straight-and-narrow path toward graduation, marriage, careers, and stable middle-class lives—lives that will probably include some form of religious affiliation.

As difficult as this struggle may be for a young woman or man in American Fork, the young Mormons who leave the comfort of places like Utah or Idaho (where they are in the majority) for places like New York City also face a tough battle. The YSA in the hip Chelsea neighborhood of Manhattan offers LDS members the same kinds of spiritual and social opportunities they have elsewhere in the country, but it is a distinctly different crowd. They are more fashionably dressed, older, and significantly more career-oriented than their counterparts out West.

Brenda Saunders grew up in a small farming community in Oregon, the sixth of twelve children. Her family has been in the church since the middle of the nineteenth century—that is, almost since its inception. When she graduated from college with a degree in accounting and fashion (she made the attractive dress she was wearing when we met), her family encouraged her to apply for a job with one of the Big Four accounting firms in New York. She wasn't sure, but she was ambitious and decided to make the move. The hours were "rough," and there was definitely an element of culture shock. She would go to the bar with her colleagues but wouldn't drink.

She decided from the outset that she would attend church every Sunday, but she found it "challenging" the first time her boss said they would be working through the weekend and she told him she'd be in on Sunday but only after she went to church for three hours first. "That was a moment where I had to stand up for myself." Saunders is about to age out of the singles ward, and while she clearly has made church a priority despite the demands of her job, she is no closer to marriage than when she arrived in New York almost a decade ago.

In New York the LDS Church faces at least three challenges when it comes to serving young singles. The first is the distraction of the career. Mark Wells, the bishop of the ward here, says that in other areas of the country, young people "work to live and in New York it seems to be flipped around." He says, "So much is required at work that when they have a day off, going to church isn't foremost on their minds." Wells says that people tell him they just need some "me time." He worries that they don't see "meditation and religion as being regenerative, but just another thing they have to do."

The single Mormon adults in New York tend to be older than their counterparts elsewhere, and they tend to have more demanding careers. So they are probably not spending as much time playing video games as the men and women whom Cory Duckworth is describing. But New York is still something of a grown-up playground, and that is the second challenge. Aside from the parties, the bars, and clubs, a couple of the women mention that it is difficult to keep Sunday holy—members of the church are not supposed to shop on the Sabbath—when they pass all sorts of great shopping even on their way to church.

Finally, you add to that the fact that most of the young people who are so focused on their jobs believe that they should put off marriage until after their careers are more established. Melissa Reidhead, who is twenty-five and works in advertising, says she has a lot of friends back home in Salt Lake City who are married now. But she doesn't feel the need to follow suit. Even her parents have told her to "have a career, have fun, do stuff, and then settle down." She says she aims to be "married by thirty."

Reidhead has clearly adopted more of a New York mind-set when it comes to marriage. Bishop Wells tries not to pressure the people in his flock too much, but he wants them to think about marriage differently than their coworkers and friends outside the church do. Wells says that he tries to advise people on the way to find the right person. It is not the way that people date in New York generally. Unfortunately, he tells me, in his ward he has noticed a lot of "perpetual dating. People date for a while and then get bored." He advocates that you "should decide what you need and then pick the right person. It's not a contest."

Reidhead comes to church most Sundays, and even if she doesn't settle down soon, it seems like the YSA ward is keeping her connected to her faith until she does. The church offers a kind of social life to LDS singles across the city, arranging events like ball games and dessert tastings that are in keeping with the Mormon way of life. Many of the New York LDS members I interview say that because maintaining an LDS lifestyle in New York is something of a hurdle, the people who do attend the ward are very strong in their faith.

From her first week in New York, Saunders says she came to the ward. "I walked in and had the feeling of, *This might be crazy New York City, but this is my church and where I want to be.*" In fact, it was the only place she could be, which may be another factor that allows young people, even those as far flung as the East Coast, to remain in the fold. There is no church shopping for LDS members as there might be with young Jews or Catholics or evangelicals or Muslims. They are assigned to a ward based on their age, marital status, and location.

Every ward has the same structure. It reads the same prayers, sings the same hymns with the same tunes. You might like some bishops better than others, but none are in the position for longer than a few years, so no cult of personality is allowed to form around them. Whereas young people in other religions might try a new religious institution every week and then decide that none really suits them, LDS young adults have the choice made for them.

The advantage of the YSA, whether in Utah or in New York, is that it can address the issues young adults face with more focus than another congregation might. From career to family to psychological problems to marriage, the people in the ward are all likely to be facing similar difficulties. The message can be tailored to them. Chris Wermly, a ward mission leader at the American Fork YSA ward, says that he is finding school to be difficult. He's trying to make decisions about his career. "Just being around people here who are going through the same situation, it's comforting because I don't feel as anxious or nervous about things. It's comforting to me that other people are in the same situation and still doing really good. So it gives me hope as well."

Through the social activities they sponsor, YSAs can also have the obvious benefit of allowing more young people to find friends and even life partners inside of the church. Finally, it can assign real leadership roles to young people, giving them the kind of responsibility that will help them see themselves and their peers as adults, not adolescents.

But this kind of age segregation does have its downsides. Lauren Winner, author of *Girl Meets God* and a professor at Duke University's divinity school, says, "Theologically [separating out the young people in their twenties and thirties] makes me break out into hives. I spend the whole rest of my life with people in my same life stage." Church should be intergenerational, says Winner. Of the claim that "people's needs are so thoroughly different at this stage of life," she says, "I find it not persuasive."

Indeed, many of the young men and women I spoke with said that they do miss seeing both older and younger people at church. Jessica Paulson told me that "it's nice to have those different perspectives from people who have had different experiences. Or because they have the simple faith of a child. There is some of that I have missed." Indeed, the YSA services that I attend seem strangely quiet—obviously the result of them lacking anyone under the age of eighteen.

Many of the members of the YSAs also feel an absence on the other end of the age spectrum. Says Taylor Jones, the American Fork ward's financial clerk, who is twenty-one, "There's only so much wisdom that a twenty-four-year-old can pass down to a twenty-two-year-old."

Many of these young people I interviewed come from large extended families who live in close proximity, and so they tend to see other generations on a regular basis, even if not at a church service. But still it is useful for them to be able to see people who are in the next stage of life. Bishop Duckworth has called to be one of his "counselors"—a leader who serves under the bishop—a young father of four. "I do think they need to see examples of people who have made the transition from being a member of this ward of all singles to being a husband and father."

But one final difficulty arises with this idea of a ward for singles under thirty: What happens when they turn thirty-one? Bishop Duckworth says that when he first took this position, he was counseling a woman in that position and he suggested that it was time for her to "move on." Says Duckworth, "She did not react positively at all. That was a mistake. I mean, I learned quickly that it is a big deal." (One suspects that reminding women they are getting older is even more problematic than reminding the men.) "It's difficult because they don't relate necessarily to people in a normal ward setting. Often times if they've been here 'til they're thirty-one, they've learned to identify more with younger people."

The LDS leadership has started to hold what they call Transition Firesides, talks with people who are about to age out of the YSAs. At these sessions, they discuss the change that is coming and how these thirty-one-year-olds can "bless the lives of people in another environment, too."

Ashley Reeves, a twenty-seven-year-old analyst for Citigroup, tells me that she is prepared for the idea of aging out of the YSA ward in Manhattan. "Age never bothers me. If I'm thirty, I'm thirty. I appreciate what they're trying to do, because when you're over thirty you're at a different point in your life." Jason Johnson is twenty-five and notes that people from the family ward have come to tell them that they found their spouses after they aged out of the YSA ward, when they were thirty-two or thirty-three.

Whether people are concerned about personally having to leave YSAs before they are married, the congregations do have a transitional vibe. Whether people age out or marry out, the congregation is one in which people cannot really put down roots for a long period of time, which makes the church community feel more like other parts of the lives of twenty- and thirty-somethings. A lot of drifting in and out of jobs, cities, living situations, and relationships takes place.

Johnson has noticed this problem. A number of his friends have aged out or left because they married. He feels he can still hang out with them, but he also feels like the YSA ward gives him a lot of chances to make new friends. Roshelle Manuela, a twenty-one-year-old college student in Utah with two full-time jobs, says she is sometimes struck by the transience of the YSA ward. But the church has made it seem like "just another step in life that we all have to take." While the people around you may be different, the messages are the same. "I'm not coming to church to be around certain types of people. I'm coming because I know this is where I need to be, this is where I belong."

When it comes to analyzing the structures of the Mormon Church, it is hard to argue with success. If the leadership says that YSAs are allowing the church to keep better track of members, to keep members on the right track, and to address more specifically the needs of young adults, well, one can't be too critical.

Getting them to take responsibility earlier as the YSAs do is definitely key to limiting the period of emerging adulthood that rightly worries many religious leaders. But there is a delicate balance here. The YSAs can also encourage some of the self-centered tendencies to which young adults may already be prone. A religious existence without older people and without younger people can start to seem very narrow and more like the rest of their lives. When Bishop Wells worries that faith does not seem to his YSA congregants to be "regenerative," he may be touching on this problem. Religious practice in the YSA ward can seem like just another social obligation.

Ultimately, though, the most important question for these wards will be whether they help young adult Mormons find a marriage partner more easily and quickly than simply attending their family's ward. While some of the members say that they feel more comfortable being single in these communities, the bishops still see it as part of their mission to pair off congregants. And simply creating a larger pool of eligible singles would probably have the desired effect.

Many American religious communities are looking for a way to get young people to engage with faith even when the cue of marriage has not happened. As young people are putting off marriage further and further into their futures, religious leaders have tried to make religious participation more feasible and desirable for single adults. From sermons to social activities, they are starting to consider ways to make singles more comfortable in their communities and less like they are in limbo.

The LDS Church probably doesn't have reason to do that—yet. The union of marriage and religion has worked well for them so far. Perhaps the creations of these discrete young adult communities will allow the church to continue on that path.

6

When No One Needs Church Anymore, How Do You Make Them Want It?

The Relevance of the Black Church in the Twenty-First Century

W HEN THE REVERED DEFOREST SOARIES attends gatherings of his fellow leaders in the Black Church, he often finds himself the youngest man in the room. Soaries, who is the senior pastor at First Baptist Church of Lincoln Gardens in Somerset, New Jersey, is sixty-two years old. The graying of the church leadership started to really concern him a few years ago, he tells me, when he learned that "the youth director for the National Baptist Convention was eighty years old."

Soaries is a man of boundless energy—perhaps the vigor of a man twenty years younger. He served as New Jersey's secretary of state under Governor Christine Todd Whitman. He has formed various nonprofits to alleviate poverty, find foster homes for children, and combat inner-city violence. And he seems determined to make a personal connection with every last one of the more than seven thousand members at Lincoln Gardens. But he does recognize that there will come a time when he will no longer be able to lead.

So a couple of years ago, he decided it was time to fire his wife. Donna Soaries was the head of the annual women's retreat ministry at Lincoln Gardens. Attendance at the retreat often tops one thousand people, which is why organizing it takes up much of the year and why being in charge of it is considered a great honor and responsibility in the congregation. But Pastor Soaries tells me that his wife had been in the role for sixteen years, and many of her friends had been serving on the committee for a similar length of time. So he asked his wife and the other ladies to please step aside and let some younger women take over.

There was some backlash, Soaries tells me. "I got a letter from someone saying that you don't want anyone with gray hair in leadership positions." But he knew that if he didn't step in, things wouldn't change. Some of the church's lay leaders, he told me, had begun to "cling to their positions. It became their personal property. They were intimidated by the idea that they might be displaced."

Soaries held a meeting with the heads of the various ministries: "I told people, 'Look around the room. Twenty years from now, we won't be here. We can't wait 'til we're too old to make this transition.'"

There was a "shawl ceremony" for the women's retreat transition, which made things seem easier and more like a natural passage was taking place. Nicole Pride, who took over the women's retreat, said the transition was "bittersweet." Pride said she was surprised when she was asked if she would take on the role. But Pastor Soaries had made clear in his public announcements that "it's time to have a new perspective, a younger perspective." She said that overall, the older members who stepped down have been "supportive," and always ask how they can help.

Lisa James, who is in charge of the young adult ministry at Lincoln Gardens, says she has noticed in other churches she is familiar with, "You have leaders who marched and heard Martin Luther King speak and they have made a difference in the community, but they are still in that mode and they're not ready to give up anything." She understands their sentiments, but she says, "It's killing the church." She says First Baptist of Lincoln Gardens is the "opposite."

In order to bring in new blood, the church has created a young adult ministry. But rather than start a separate young adult worship service or a parallel set of activities for young adults, Lincoln Gardens has started a group called Fusion, whose mission is to "fuse" young adults into the already existing ministries—"to have young adults go into different ministries in the church and utilize and apply their faith there." The idea is that, when the time comes, the young adults will be well equipped to take over the ministries. For some endeavors, like the women's retreat, that time has already arrived. But for others, the young adults are fully participating members, learning the ropes before taking on leadership roles. Right now young adults are helping to lead the new members' ministry as well as the marriage ministry.

James explains to her peers that "the church is looking at you, and the deacons see you there. It may be weird for you to picture it now, but you will be the leaders. You have a responsibility not only to yourselves but to God to serve God in a manner God has called you to."

While being more intentional about hiring younger people is easy—the bulk of the Lincoln Gardens staff now is between the ages of twenty-five and forty—it is much more difficult with lay leaders who are volunteering. How old should they be? As we are living longer, healthier lives, it is not at all hard to imagine that people in their seventies and eighties will start to make up the bulk of the church leadership.

In an interview with *Christianity Today* in the spring of 2013, megachurch pastor Rick Warren was asked, "Who's going to get your job when you retire?" He explained that he launched a plan to hand over the church to younger leadership a long time ago. "When I started Saddleback in 1980, I announced that I was going to give forty years to the church, then turn it over to younger leadership. At sixty-five, I'll still have more energy than any young guy. [But] they need a new face. I have seven more years at Saddleback. It's no secret." He explained that he doesn't even manage

Saddleback anymore. It's the Timothy generation, everybody under forty, that is now leading the church.

Those under forty are named the "Timothy generation" because so many of the apostle Paul's words were addressed to Timothy. Paul told the Philippians about Timothy, "I have no one else of kindred spirit who will genuinely be concerned for your welfare" (Phil. 2:20 NASB). Paul added, "But you know of his proven worth, that he served with me in the furtherance of the gospel like a child serving his father" (v. 22).

Unfortunately, many sixty- and seventy-somethings see the Timothy generation as permanent children. Getting boomers to give up their power to the Timothy generation is difficult, as anyone on a university faculty might attest. But this issue is perhaps even more pressing for the Black Church. The generation that is now holding on is the generation that led the civil rights movement. The church provided the members of this generation with a political, social, and religious identity—and the members in turn provided the church with a kind of energy the likes of which, to be honest, might not be seen again for some time. For this generation to hand the reins to young adults might be more than a matter of strategic planning. It will be a matter of soul searching.

Eric McDaniels, a professor at the University of Texas at Austin who has studied the history of the Black Church, notes that the "pinnacle of [its] success was the civil rights movement." But that success actually "made the church much less important."

For blacks, he says, the church "used to be a semi-involuntary institution. Even nonreligious blacks went to church because it was the center of social life," and there were few alternatives. But the church has been a victim of its own success. While African Americans are still more religious than any other ethnic group in America, McDaniels says they are "beginning to move away from organized religion."

Atheism among blacks has risen from 6 percent in 1990 to 11 percent in 2008, according to a Pew Survey. Support groups for black atheists have begun to form around the country. Richard Peacock, the founder of a group called the Black Nonbelievers of Metro Orlando, told the *Orlando Sentinel* that being a black atheist is actually more difficult than being an atheist of another race. "The black church is so much a part of black life, heritage and culture . . . It's assumed that even if you aren't going to church, it's part of your DNA."

In some cases, young adults are choosing other types of houses of worship, which is to say, some are simply joining multiracial churches instead of identifiably black ones. They go to school and work and live in neighborhoods with people of other races. Why not church?

For the most part, this choice does not seem like a popular one. According to the 2009 National Congregations Study, the percentage of congregations with more than 80 percent white participation dropped from 72 percent to 63 percent between 1998 and 2007. But most of this shift did not occur as a result of African Americans changing churches. Rather these numbers reflect Catholic parishes receiving significant populations of immigrants, particularly Hispanic ones. And many of those congregations are undergoing a kind of ethnic shift; that is, they are not going to remain multiracial. Rather, they will have a different majority race soon.

Indeed, most of the Black Church leaders and parishioners I interviewed did not report that young adults were leaving for multiracial churches, and few had adopted a new mind-set of unbelief. Rather, it seems that many twenty- or thirty-something young adults—like their peers in other races—are simply dropping out.

Geography is clearly playing a role. Many black churches remain in the inner cities, while middle-class and even working-class blacks are finding their way to the suburbs. The church is missing just the people it needs in order to be successful. McDaniels says they are losing "college-educated, white-collar-job people. They have a lot of resources and talent."

More importantly, McDaniels says that something about the style of the traditional African American church can be a turnoff to younger people. The church, he says, has a "classically authoritarian structure," which means not only a kind of old-time religion unafraid of mentioning the devil and hell, but it also means that the pastor is the one in charge. "He was usually the best-educated person in the community and the one who earned the highest income." So he was universally respected and his words were heeded. Now, notes McDaniels, "There are many people walking into church with a higher income, and that authoritarian thing doesn't work as well."

Indeed, the fact that so many other professions are open to blacks now that weren't possibilities fifty years ago has also meant that the church has had trouble recruiting well-qualified candidates for the ministry. So the congregation is getting better-educated and wealthier while the clergy may be headed in the opposite direction, relatively speaking.

First Baptist of Lincoln Gardens is located in a New Jersey suburb. Its immediate neighborhood looks a little run-down, but it is only a couple of miles from Rutgers University and headquarters of some major corporations like Johnson & Johnson. The crowd there is decidedly mixed in terms of class. But regardless of whether they are professionals or chronically unemployed, almost all of the young adults who attend mention the way that Pastor Soaries's sermons are "relatable."

While Soaries has a degree from Fordham and Princeton Theological Seminary, he does not talk down to his congregation. Arthur Thomas finds Pastor Soaries "inspirational. I felt that he had a tremendous anointing, you know, his ability to deliver biblical principles in a practical manner." Thomas attended church as a child, but then stopped for what he calls "a significant period of time." He came back five years ago or so, at the age of thirty, and he says it was the pastor who drew him in.

Just like one can find new meanings in biblical passages by

reading them again and again, Thomas finds himself going back to the pastor's messages. "They apply to more areas of your life than the original theme may have suggested."

Whitney Barno, who is twenty-five and works in marketing, came up to New Jersey after college from her home in South Carolina. She wanted a support system here, so she began looking at different churches. The atmosphere of First Baptist of Lincoln Gardens appealed to her because it seemed more "progressive." Many mention the appeal of the church's social gospel mission, but people return again and again to the messages of Pastor Soaries.

Barno tells me, "I thought the preaching was very relatable—the pastor kind of connecting your everyday life back to the Word." She says she has been encouraged not only to listen on Sundays but to do her own exploration, "to dig a little deeper" inside herself. She is pleased that the underlying message is "not hard to obtain. It's something that connects to everyday life."

The fact that many people used the term "relatable" in describing Pastor Soaries's sermons suggests that this is not the classic authoritarian model for a black church. The church's weekly Bible study is another example of what congregants call the "relevance" of the church to their lives.

Lisa James begins each Tuesday night meeting with a hymn. The song "Oh How I Love Jesus," which was composed in 1855, doesn't exactly sound very energetic on the evening I attend. Minister James tells the group that she will deliver a homily and then Arthur Thomas will offer a reflection. "It sounds like the old church, huh?" she jokes.

But the thirty people who are assembled look at the passage they are supposed to discuss and immediately join in. And the discussion, it's true, is not the type that would take place in the old church. Minister James talks about the passage starting at Mark 12:31, in which Jesus says to love your neighbor as yourself, and compares the biblical understanding of love with the understanding presented in pop culture. She moves quickly from Rihanna to

Soulchild. The Bruno Mars song "Locked Out of Heaven" suggests that sex is paradise, she tells the group, and asks what they think of that.

The young men and women—interestingly there are an almost equal number of them—discuss the pressures of their lives and how they are coping. One has changed her ringtone to a gospel song. Another one has had a hard time adjusting to the concept of "unconditional love" in the Bible. "We're so used to buying people's acceptance with material goods." A young woman says she has started a journal for writing her thoughts about loving God. A man says he always had to have the "hottest shorties" in order to impress other people, but he realized that God loves him regardless. "You can put your heart in his hands."

This is not exactly ground-breaking stuff for a church in the twenty-first century. In fact, one could easily imagine these conversations taking place in a teen Bible study in other, more liberal churches. But perhaps because black churches have such a traditional feel, the young adults in this group appreciated the fact that Minister James seemed to have an interest in discussing their "real-world" problems.

There are plenty of historical reasons why the shift toward a more "relevant" form of worship and study has taken longer to arrive in the Black Church. In his book *The Juvenilization of American Christianity*, Thomas Bergler notes that in the mid-twentieth century, some leaders wanted to make the church more welcoming to young people. Just as other Catholic and Protestant churches had begun to change their worship style to appeal to a younger generation—through more modern music, for instance—some black clergy wanted to do the same.

At the First Baptist Church of Nashville, for instance, Rev. Kelly Miller Smith "worried that the emphasis on heaven and consolation in old-time religion might alienate young people." But Smith was going against the grain. Most black churches took longer to focus on youth specifically, notes Bergler. For one thing, the racial injustices they faced "forced every young person to realize that some things were more important than fun and entertainment."

Instead, Black Church leaders tried to maintain an aura of respectability, even at the risk of turning off the younger generation. The church leaders saw themselves as the face of a political movement and didn't want to do anything to endanger that. But as the civil rights movement heated up and matters became more desperate and violent in the 1960s, many young African Americans felt that the church was insufficient or even unnecessary. As one young leader put it, "No prayer is necessary to open this meeting. We shall be concerned with social problems, and it is too late for God or the church to pretend to have any concern. We know better." When Stokely Carmichael replaced John Lewis as the head of the Student Non-Violent Coordinating Committee in 1966, he called Lewis a "Christ-loving damn fool."

In many ways, it seems, history conspired to keep black churches more traditional in style and substance than many white ones, a point that is visible in any number of ways today. People still tend to dress up more for church in the African American community. Black views on social issues like gay marriage tend to be more conservative. They are theologically conservative, too; black Protestants are more likely than most other religious groups in America to believe in only a single path to salvation. According to the 2008 Pew Religious Landscape survey, "Among black Protestants, 49 percent take the view that many religions lead to everlasting life, while 45 percent see theirs as the one, true faith." Black Protestants are also more likely to believe in heaven (91 percent) and hell (82 percent) than any other religious group in America, according to the survey.

But these theological views may not comport with the worldviews of twenty- and thirty-something African Americans. Charles Corpening, the chairman of the Lincoln Gardens church's board of trustees, acts as a kind of mentor to many young adults at the church. He tells me that "many churches and religious leaders haven't really focused on keeping the faith relevant for young people." Corpening, who was raised in poverty by a single mother but managed to get a scholarship to Princeton and become a successful businessman, notes the rise of the self-help industry and the popularity of self-help books in the community. But "who is a better life coach than God?" he asks.

Corpening believes that the community has dug itself into this hole with young adults. He believes that they are "coddled" and that adults in their lives don't give them enough responsibility. The average age of church trustees used to be in the sixties. Now it's in the fifties, and Corpening says he's trying to move it down further. But he also believes that young adults need to take more control in their own lives, and that will ultimately translate into taking a greater role in the church.

A few years ago, Pastor Soaries launched a program called D-free. The "D" stands for "debt," and the pastor is trying to give everyone in the congregation the wherewithal to be financially independent. He offers his congregants education about everything from student loans to life insurance to mortgages that they need in order to live lives free from what he calls the "slavery" of debt. In 2011, he published a book called *D-Free*, which explains the importance of Christians being financially literate.

While the economic messages were intended for all generations, many of the young adults I spoke with told me that they felt it had special resonance for them. "From where I grew up," says Arthur Thomas, "I just noticed the impact that financial destitution has on so many people's lives. It becomes everything for them, and it strips them away from being able to reach their God-given purpose." Thomas, who used to work on Wall Street but now runs a nonprofit, says he has tried to share with other people the D-free message.

Whitney Barno says that she "did not pay much attention" to her finances before she started attending Lincoln Gardens. She paid her bills, but she was not thinking about saving for the future.

But since coming here, she says, she has realized that planning financially—including saving and tithing—"ties into trying to be a better person in every aspect of your life." Minister James tells me it's not uncommon in her community for women "to drop $150 a week on getting their hair done," but they don't think about insurance or savings—and few churches talk about those things.

Latasha Owens wished she had heard Pastor Soaries's message of financial stewardship earlier in her life. Now, she says, she is trying "to correct some of the mistakes she has made." Often, she says, her generation "just does what our parents did when it comes to money."

Nicole Pride tells a similar story. "I was the stupid person who applied for every credit card." She thinks a lot of recent college grads are burdened by student loans they're trying to pay off, and if they're lucky enough to have jobs, they're not entirely sure how to spend their salaries.

Not many churches get into the nitty-gritty of money management the way Lincoln Gardens does. Not only do weekly classes address these issues, but Soaries regularly discusses in his sermons being a good steward of your money.

One Sunday morning I arrive early for the 9 a.m. service. (The church holds about two thousand people at a time, and there are three services each Sunday.) With the help of the ushers, people are finding seats. Everyone is dressed to the nines, and the ladies are keeping cool with the small fans they've been given. The pastor is welcoming a friend, a fellow clergyman who runs a church in Liberia. Pastor Soaries explains the program at Providence Baptist Church in Monrovia to rehabilitate former child soldiers. He tells the congregation that he has "made a commitment from Lincoln Gardens to help the Liberian church." While most members of Lincoln Gardens are not wealthy, they have been extraordinarily generous in their tithing. For the church's seventy-fifth anniversary, they have set a goal of raising $75,000.

Whereas most religious institutions' capital campaigns are

intended to fund expansions or upgrades of their facilities, the leaders of Lincoln Gardens say their goal is to pay off the church's mortgage in ten years.

"This is not about fund-raising or budget building or even about tithing," says Pastor Soaries. "This is about your attitude toward all of life." He tells the assembled men and women, "We need to picture ourselves as tenants in God's universe, to live out the biblical image of stewardship." He repeats several times the idea, "I will not give God anything that costs me nothing," and he instructs the congregation, "God doesn't want your resources—he already owns everything. He wants your heart." These messages seem to hold a particular appeal for young people. Many of them have been turned off by showy displays of wealth at other churches and the sense that those who have the most money to throw around are the most valued members of the community.

In fact, some people, including Pastor Soaries, worry about the way that leaders in the black community—religious leaders and politicians—send exactly the wrong message about money and consumption. I ran into Pastor Soaries shortly after Jesse Jackson Jr., the former Illinois congressman, pleaded guilty to using $750,000 worth of campaign funds for personal use. "A $43,000 Rolex?" Soaries exclaimed with outrage regarding the congressman's spending habits. "I hope that watch does more than tell time."

Many of the young adults interviewed are disappointed by some of the other church leaders with whom they have come into contact. Anthony Jefferson grew up in New Jersey, where his grandmother would take him to a pentecostal church every week. But he stopped going by the time he was a teenager. He says that many of the churches he and his friends have tried out have turned them off because of what he calls the "hypocrisy" both in the pews and in the pulpit. The congregation is struggling financially, he explains, while the pastor and his wife are "wearing Gucci shoes."

The prosperity gospel—the theory that God wants us all to be wealthy and we need only follow the instructions of the pastor in order to achieve that wealth—is commonly preached in black churches. But it may be turning off many young adults. As Eric McDaniels notes, the prosperity gospel tends to "fall apart during recessions." He says that during boom years, "People want a justification for why there is a boom and that they can be wealthy, too."

Pastor Soaries published an article in the *Wall Street Journal* criticizing the prosperity gospel. He said, "When leaders of this movement assert that God wants everyone to be wealthy and that riches are the automatic outcome for all faithful believers, we should all be suspicious. Teaching that desire for more material possessions is a sign of one's religious piety is simply offering a justification for crass consumerism. Prosperity theology elevates greed to a virtue instead of leaving it as one of the seven deadly sins."

But he explains that many church leaders use prosperity theology in order to justify their own conspicuous consumption. Soaries writes, "Of course, it is much easier for clergy to preach this gospel when they are living proof that the 'system' works. Hence the celebrity-like lifestyles of so many religious leaders. The fact that the people most likely to do well in the prosperity gospel movement are the people at the top suggests that it is all an ecclesiastical pyramid scheme."

More than one young person at Lincoln Gardens told me that they had stayed away from church for a while because they either felt that people who go to church were "hypocrites" or, relatedly, that they themselves would feel like hypocrites if they went to church given that they were not living godly lives. "In your mind," says Jefferson, "you associate church with doing 100 percent right and no wrong. You feel like it will be okay to go to church when you're ready to do right with your life." If your life isn't right and you go to church, you will feel like a hypocrite, he tells me.

Nyle Fort, the twenty-two-year-old youth pastor at Lincoln

Gardens, agrees with that assessment. Most young adults see the church as hypocritical, according to Fort. And they also do not see the connection "between faith and reality." Not only is the church a place that welcomes sinners, but faith is the basis for doing good in the real world, for social action. "When that connection is made, it becomes real."

Interestingly, Fort says that the Black Church has "gotten away from the social gospel message of Martin Luther King and others who connected how people live every day and how they see God." He tells me, "I don't think we do a good enough job of getting that message out."

Of all the places for the social gospel to fall away, observers might not expect the Black Church to be high on the list. After all, the social gospel was thought to be largely responsible for the participation of white liberal churches in the civil rights movement.

But as Princeton University professor Robert Wuthnow points out, whether churches embraced the social gospel depended much more on their location than on what race of people belonged to them. Northern churches were more likely to embrace it, while southern churches leaned "in a Pentecostal direction." But even in the Northeast, black churches still seem to be more theologically conservative—not as socially progressive as churches dominated by whites.

In many ways, Lincoln Gardens is an atypical black church. Its pastor has rejected the prosperity gospel and regularly criticizes leaders in the black community for the way they think about consumption and what he sees as their misguided attempt to use the legacy of the civil rights movement to further their political agendas today. But Lincoln Gardens is very much facing the same kinds of issues as other black churches. It is straddling a kind of class divide, with some members who are professionals and others coming from nearby working-class neighborhoods.

Pastor Soaries seems to have found a way to reach young adults from a variety of backgrounds. His commitment to offering relatable messages (especially messages about financial stewardship) has meant that the millennial generation feels welcome at Lincoln Gardens, and Pastor Soaries has taken matters further. He is pushing these twenty- and thirty-somethings into leadership positions by pushing his own generation out of them.

Like many other religious communities in America, the Black Church has to face a new social landscape in which going to church is no longer considered a given. Achieving professional and social respectability without setting foot inside a religious institution is entirely possible. And for blacks who are looking for ways to become active in their communities, plenty of other outlets for their energies are available these days.

So Black Church leaders have slowly returned to the drawing board to figure out what about belonging to a faith community should be attractive to young adults. The prosperity gospel, with its promise of great wealth for those who believe, will always appeal to some. But do we really want to make the success of our religious institutions subject to the vagaries of the economy? Pastor Soaries is offering a different route. It is a harder one theologically, with less in the way of immediate gratification, but the emphasis on service certainly appeals to this younger generation. And as the black community grows more educated and more economically mobile, offering young people a less superficial understanding of faith and a greater sense of responsibility to others will make them the kind of pillars in the community that their parents and grandparents once were.

7

The End of Sheep Stealing

How Churches Can Collaborate to Bring
Twenty-Somethings Back into the Fold

O N   A   P L E A S A N T   spring evening in downtown Charlotte, North Carolina, a crowd of well-dressed young people were streaming into a beautifully adorned United Methodist Church. They climbed the stone stairs toward one of three open doors and were greeted at the top by men and women (mostly in their twenties) beckoning them in and directing them where to sit.

By the time the lights dimmed for the Christian rock band Gungor (and the opening act, The Brilliance), the capacity crowd numbered more than six hundred. Some were sitting with groups of friends. Others came as couples or alone, but seemed to be quickly absorbed into conversations with strangers nearby. The audience was not, by and large, made up of members of United Methodist.

Rather, the mostly single professionals and students were brought here by Charlotte ONE, a collaboration of forty or so area churches trying to reach this demographic. "Collaborative" is the key word this evening: David Hickman, the lead visionary of Charlotte ONE, repeats the word for the audience several times and even has them repeat it back to him. He thanks all of the churches that have made the event possible and explains that the goal of Charlotte ONE is to "reintroduce a generation to Christ and his bride, the church."

Before the "reintroduction" begins, he asks the members of the audience to "center yourself and tell God you're here." He offers a prayer to God: "I want to thank you that you're not a distant deity, to thank you for art and music. And to thank you for this gathering, across denominational lines." The group takes its motivation from Jesus's words in John 17:23: "Let them be one, so that the world may know that you sent me and loved them even as much as you have loved me."

Many of the more than seven hundred churches in this area have tried to run so-called young adult ministries—but with little success. James Michael Smith, one of the several pastors present at the launch of Charlotte ONE, tells me that a common problem is the return on investment: "Young adults are the least reliable, the most mobile, and they don't give financially either." But it's not just the fact that they don't want to commit in the long term, by giving what leaders refer to as "time, talent, and treasure." In order even to get them in the door, Smith adds, churches have to offer the "wow factor."

Young people, especially those who went to a college with a Campus Crusade or other well-funded university ministry, are used to great music, performances with high production values, and charismatic preachers. They are accustomed to groups that cater to their musical, emotional, and intellectual experiences. When these students leave college, they expect the situation to remain the same. But churches—even large churches—often don't have the kind of resources to run programs with the wow factor. Those churches that do have the money feel it is better spent on programming for children or families, who will make a real commitment to the church in the long run.

But at least a few of the Christian leaders in Charlotte were not quite ready to throw in the towel. They wanted to give young adults something—a kind of gateway from their college experiences into the city's churches. They wanted it to seem like a natural transition from a school—something fun and social, yet substantive.

Many of the leaders of Charlotte ONE tell me that they want to make sure that young adults would not feel "embarrassed" bringing their friends to the events. As Smith explained, "We're going to intentionally try to do something excellent that people will want to come to. We're going to avoid the cringe factor." If a friend sits through it and finds that it is not up to the standards of a college ministry, for instance, that would be "counterproductive."

But in addition to being cool, Smith says the goal was to make sure the messages had wisdom. They wanted their sermons and performances not only to be "tops in terms of popularity but in terms of depth, in terms of substance." He says the founders of Charlotte ONE "wanted people to not only hear a motivational talk by someone who is a Christian but to actually hear the message of the gospel, the message of the Old Testament—so that they're experiencing Christianity, rather than a sort of Joel Osteen 'Life is what you make of it' approach."

Finding that sweet spot between deep religious messages that sound cool and Christianity that seems like it comes from a sappy self-help book is not easy. On the one hand, young adults value relevance in sermons (as we saw at First Baptist of Lincoln Gardens in chapter 6). They want information they can use in their daily lives. But, on the other hand, they don't want to be talked down to, and many of them appreciate substance in their religious services.

Charlotte ONE seems to have struck that balance. A number of attendees mention to me that they have particularly enjoyed a series of sermons about relationships. "The messages were geared toward our age group," says Leigh Justice, a young woman who started attending a few months ago. "They did a series on how you should be in the single life, how you should be when you start dating, how you should be when you're married, and how these things should look in a Christian lifestyle." She says, "It was all very applicable."

Other people were touched by a message about depression. Smith gave that talk, focusing particular attention on Psalm 88, which ends with the following passage: "Your wrath has swept over me; your terrors have destroyed me. All day long they surround me like a flood; they have completely engulfed me. You have taken from me friend and neighbor—darkness is my closest friend." Smith says there wasn't a huge turnout for that week's event—only three or four hundred people. But many people came up to him afterward to tell him how much they were affected by the message. Clearly many of the attendees had experienced clinical depression or a kind of dark night of the soul. Both groups were touched by his words.

Other people mention to me that they have liked the messages about the historical veracity of Christianity. Some members of Charlotte ONE's leadership worry that the religious experience offered by college ministry (and youth ministry before it) is not doing a good enough job answering people's intellectual questions about Christianity, and Charlotte ONE is hoping to step into that role.

Mandy Schmitt moved to Charlotte from Germany to live with some extended family. She is new in her faith and appreciates the "topics we can relate to." But she also says she "loves to go to church to learn history."

But the leaders of Charlotte ONE also have to tread lightly. Ryan Blalock, who works at the Myers Park United Methodist Church, says that young adults don't like listening to sermons—at least in the traditional sense. "What I've noticed," he tells me, "is that people aren't that drawn to a sermon where there's one person speaking to everybody else. People want to be involved. People want to have their voice heard."

The Charlotte ONE speakers and their messages must be chosen very carefully. For one thing, the group of churches that sponsor the organization come from mainline and evangelical denominations. David Hickman tells me that while Charlotte ONE would be considered more evangelical in its outlook (its positions are broadly in line with the National Association of Evangelicals, a liberal-leaning evangelical group), many of the mainline churches feel comfortable being a part of it.

Of the other pastors who support Charlotte ONE, Hickman says, "We've built a friendship and trust. They know that I'm not going to do anything that is going to embarrass them or their mission." He says, "Do we agree on everything? No. Do they tell me what I can teach on? No. Do I tell them what they can teach on? No." Charlotte ONE's speakers generally steer clear of hot-button political topics like abortion and gay marriage, and they also avoid topics that divide denominations like baptism or election. Schmitt says she likes that Charlotte ONE doesn't "get into the nitty-gritty," but focuses on "God and Jesus and that he loves us." She depends on her own church to deal with more of the theological details.

The collaboration of mainline and evangelical churches these days is rare, to say the least, which may signal at least a little bit of desperation on the part of the mainline churches. A 2009 report from Barna found that since the 1950s, the number of mainline churches has declined from eighty thousand to about seventy-two thousand. Moreover, in the decade prior to the survey, there was a "22 percent drop in the percentage of adults attending mainline congregations who have children under the age of 18 living in their home." And finally, while "young adults (25 or younger) are 6 percent of the national population, they are just one-third as many (2 percent) of all adults attending mainline churches."

Because of the care that Charlotte ONE has taken in choosing messages that are compatible with the missions of all of its sponsoring churches, the effort to have evangelicals and mainliners collaborate seems to be working.

The significance of denominational lines in American Protestantism has been severely diminished in recent decades. Indeed, religious affiliation in general has been dropping, even among people who engage in religious practices. According to data from the Pew Forum on Religion and Public Life, in 2007, 60 percent of people who said they seldom or never attend religious services still identified themselves with a particular religious group. By 2012, that number fell to 50 percent.

The decline of religious affiliation has resulted in more church hopping as people find that the Methodist church is not so different from the Baptist church across the street anymore. (And one may have a more dynamic pastor or a better early childhood program.) The move away from affiliation has resulted in the tremendous growth of so-called nondenominational churches. Finally, it has also allowed for greater cooperation among different churches, and Charlotte ONE is aiming to be a part of that ecumenical trend.

In part, this move has been out of necessity. The need for cooperation is particularly strong with regard to engaging young adults. James Michael Smith, a pastor at the Good Shepherd United Methodist Church in Charlotte, recalls his frustration trying to draw twenty-somethings to his church. "We'd say, all right, we're going to do a service. We're going to gear it toward young adults. We'll advertise it. The first week, we'd get a decent crowd." But then, says Smith, things went downhill. "The next week it would be about half that and the next week it would be half of that." He says the problem was that "everything would just fizzle after the newness wore off." The same few people would continue to come back, but then, he says, "It was sort of a drain on the church resources."

A few years ago, several of the large area churches simply shut down their young adult programs within a few months of each other. Smith says that he and his colleagues had all tried various approaches—small Bible studies, field trips to ball games, large concert events. But basically, he concluded, "We were all trying to reinvent the wheel."

The wow factor—expensive bands, charismatic preachers, elaborate social events—doesn't come cheap. At Carmel Baptist Church, pastor Jay Hancock found that the young adults in his flock were looking for a "midweek experience." The young adult ministry decided that for four weeks they would forgo their budget for all other activities and just meet Tuesday nights, and "have great speakers or a great band so you get a good worship connection."

It worked. The church drew many people beyond their own congregation. About one hundred people showed up the first week. By the fourth week, they had 250. Despite the success, they didn't have the money to continue. But a group of young pastors around the city heard about what was going on at Carmel Baptist, and they wanted to support the effort, too. The group raised some money and chose David Hickman, a local pastor, as its leader.

At the beginning, Hickman asked the group, "Is this for Carmel Baptist? Does this work only as long as it's there??"

Hancock's answer was no. He didn't care where this group met so long as it continued to draw this crowd. Charlotte ONE has been hosted by a few different churches now in different parts of the sprawling metropolis. "This is a gift to the city," Hancock said. And he turned out to be right. In a survey of more than three hundred Charlotte ONE participants, 91 percent said the program "made [me] feel more comfortable living in Charlotte" and three-quarters said that "Charlotte ONE or the connections [I've] made through it, influenced [me] to continue to live in the Charlotte area."

Charlotte can feel like a transient place. Several people I interviewed told me that they never meet anyone who is actually *from* the city. Charlotte is the hub for Wells Fargo and some other large banks, and plenty of young people move there right after college for work. In some ways the Charlotte ONE program embraces that transience. The leaders estimate probably 100 percent turnover every four years or so. They believe that people do form long-term friendships through the program, but mostly the leaders just see it as a conduit for getting people into a real church community.

"Outreach" is the word on the tips of so many religious leaders' tongues these days. But the question of how to extend an institution's influence as far as possible while still serving those in the community is a difficult task both spiritually and financially.

"Charlotte ONE has always had a heart for the prodigal son," says Hickman. "Someone who had at some point in their lives some type of either intellectual or feelings-based experience with things of faith—God, religion, service—that really sets a deep place in them and it never really developed." And now, says Hickman, "They find themselves in Charlotte, they don't know anybody." He worries that the young adults who move to Charlotte "are in a kind of distant country where a lot of them are selling themselves out to things that are really draining them of life. So it's that lonely, isolated, insecure, young working professional" whom the group is going after.

Drew Gregory had a more extreme version of that experience. He grew up in Atlanta as the son of two ministers. But then he strayed. He hung out with some guys in college who were into "partying and drugs." He says he would go and "try to do things that everyone says will make you happy, but you get deeper into something and you realize that the people you're hanging out with are making you miserable." He realized that he was "just hurting himself." He says he didn't exactly "hit bottom, but I realized where this was going."

Gregory started attending Charlotte ONE a few years ago and has also become involved in a local church and various service projects. He now brings some of his old friends to Charlotte ONE. "It's hard to sit there because you know they're feeling really conflicted about all the things that they do." He says they resist giving up their patterns of drinking and drugs and partying. Sometimes they don't come with him for a long time. "But I know it's made an impact on their lives. One day they may come back around because of that. It's planting seeds."

Yelena Pecheny grew up in Charlotte but went away to school. She was involved in Campus Crusade and had a tight group of friends, but when she moved back to Charlotte for a job in marketing, she says it was "more difficult to find fellowship." She was suddenly no longer in the "bubble" of college life. She ended up at Charlotte ONE and then found a local pentecostal church to attend. She has done some service work through her church and for the Ronald McDonald House. But Charlotte ONE, she says, has helped her make more personal connections. As a result, Yelena says, she is more inclined to "look for work here or go back to school here." In the last few months she realizes that she has "invested so much" in the Charlotte community.

Charlotte has the distinction (at least anecdotally speaking) of having more churches per capita than any other city in the United States, which may be both a blessing and a curse. (It's hard to measure such things. New churches are always launching with just a dozen people or so, and old ones fade away slowly.)

A number of the young people I talked to seemed inclined to find a church when they came to Charlotte. But once they started their search, they just kept jumping from one to another. Jenna Lagerman grew up in an evangelical Presbyterian church in Detroit and came to Charlotte for her first job after college. Here she found a "sea of churches." She met one person at a tennis match who invited her to church. She went a few times but then realized "the beliefs . . . were a little off from what I grew up with."

So she tried a few more. She would go on Sunday mornings. She would attend their small groups, but she says, "I had a really hard time connecting."

A friend from home recommended she try Charlotte ONE. "I love it," Lagerman says. "It's a great service, with awesome music— just like my church in Michigan." She found the atmosphere to be "upbeat." A month after attending her first service, she decided to volunteer as a greeter. "The leader [of the volunteers] was super friendly," she recalls. The group would meet on weekends for service projects. And through Charlotte ONE she found the church she belongs to now. In addition to providing her with the kind of close-knit community she was looking for, Charlotte ONE also helped to direct her to a church that would become a more permanent home.

Leigh Justice tells a similar story. She went to a Presbyterian church when she was a kid. But then her parents switched to a Methodist church, and her friends attended the local Baptist church. "I grew up pretty much across denominations," she tells me. So it's not surprising that when she came to Charlotte she wasn't sure what she wanted. She started attending Elevation Church, a fast-growing multisite Baptist church in the area, but then decided it was too big and impersonal. She then attended Center City Church, which only has about one hundred members. Friends from Charlotte ONE tried to help her find the right place.

Aside from the aversion that many millennials seem to have affiliating themselves with institutions, they also seem to suffer from something psychologists call the paradox of choice. In a famous experiment, supermarket customers were offered the choice of twenty-four types of jam while others were offered only six types. Customers in both scenarios sampled the same number of jams. But only 3 percent of the former decided to purchase any jam, compared with 30 percent of the latter.

When people are offered too many choices, they may, in other words, simply throw up their arms and walk out of the store. The same dynamic may be at work in our religious marketplace. One may be willing to sample the same number of churches regardless of how many there are in a given area, but one may also be less willing to commit. Perhaps consumers of jam or religion think that they will not ultimately be as happy with their choice because they will always think there was something better out there.

Charlotte ONE is not supposed to replace church. It meets only twenty-eight weeks of the year, never on Sundays. Charlotte ONE does not perform baptisms, weddings, or funerals, or offer Communion. No single pastor is in charge. Instead Charlotte ONE's organizers see it as a kind of "funnel," taking in a wide swath of people and trying to pour them out in the right direction. On the sidewalk outside of Charlotte ONE events is a tent where volunteers show newcomers a map of the area with the collaborating churches pinpointed on it. The group also holds at least two "church fairs" annually to introduce young people to area churches.

Rather than simply throw people into a sea of churches, Charlotte ONE tries to offer boats that take them to a particular island. Its organizers try to find out what young people are looking for in a church and match them with an institution that suits their spiritual needs.

Feedback suggests that the effort is meeting its objectives. In one survey, 98 percent of attendees said the program had "enriched [their] personal relationship with Jesus Christ," and 42 percent said that it had helped them "connect . . . to local churches." Another measure of success is that other religious communities are looking to reproduce the experience. Phoenix ONE launched recently, and other communities, like Richmond, Virginia, are also exploring the possibility.

Actually Charlotte ONE allows attendees to have it both ways. Many young adults are interested in joining smaller churches. Some sociologists suggest that megachurches are a phenomenon of the baby boom generation. These large congregations were generally founded by boomer pastors who were able to draw in fast-growing suburban populations. But now that the housing bubble has burst and the founding pastors are starting to retire, many observers are wondering whether that model will be sustainable. As Skye Jethani, the senior editor of *Leadership Journal*, wrote for the Huffington Post, "A megachurch located in a growing suburb in 1990 may no longer find itself in the same demographic soup that ignited its rise to mega-ness."

As much as the mega-ness often holds little appeal for young adults, for people in their twenties and thirties who are interested in dating and marriage, going to a small church has a real downside—the small number of people in the dating pool. Attending Charlotte ONE, however, can make up for that.

Ryan Blalock, who worked in the technology sector for AT&T and before that for Google, says that many people come to

Charlotte ONE "to meet other single people." And there's nothing wrong with that, he tells me. "It brings them in. They're listening to the message. Presence is 90 percent of the battle."

Singles might even feel more comfortable at Charlotte ONE than at a traditional church setting where the message might be geared more toward married couples and families. After the event, a lot of attendees go out for drinks or coffee. Charlotte ONE participants introduce each other to potential dates, and the circle of young adult Christians expands.

In some ways, it is easy to see why pastors would be giddy at the idea of a Charlotte ONE arrangement. It relieves them of having to compete for members by spending lots of money and banging their heads against the wall trying to figure out the best way to form a young adult ministry. Many religious leaders simply feel like they want to get out of the entertainment competition and return to real ministry. If young people can find a cool event and fun people to hang out with on Tuesday nights, maybe they won't need that as much from their own church.

But pastors worry that even offering the wow factor to young people through Charlotte ONE encourages them to think about the "attractional church," the kind of place you go for entertainment but not for any long-term commitment.

Rob Kelly, who is also on the staff at Carmel Baptist, believes that Christian leaders have actually dug themselves into this hole. He says it begins with the way that churches teach children. "We've taken a lot of the responsibility away from parents. They come, drop their kids off, and expect their kids in Sunday school to be entertained—to have a really cool show and a good program where they're taught a nice Bible lesson." Then in junior high school and high school they also come to expect something "cool." By the time they have gone through college ministry, says Kelly, he believes that people begin to "worship worship rather than worship God . . . They want to come to an experience rather than come to what the experience is pointing you toward."

By that point, though, many of the adult leaders feel their hands are tied. So the best thing they can do is say that Charlotte ONE will have those kinds of cool experiences. But Charlotte ONE will encourage you to go to church, and the church doesn't need to have those experiences. "In a perfect world," says Kelly, "Charlotte ONE wouldn't exist."

It's an interesting notion—the idea that we will run one last wow program so that we don't have to run anymore afterward. People use Charlotte ONE in order to finally find a group of friends and an institution that allows them to settle into life as adult Christians, as mature members of a community who give as much as they take. The pastors who support Charlotte ONE seem to think it is worth their churches' financial contributions. Many have received a small influx of young adults through the program. And most Charlotte ONE people I've spoken to do not seem inclined to stay with it for more than a couple of years. They do want to get more involved with a real church and have a relationship with a pastor.

But the other unique aspect of Charlotte ONE is its collaborative nature, which many of the young adults clearly find attractive. Polls show that young people are less inclined to affiliate with a particular denomination. About 20 percent of Americans now claim no religious affiliation, according to a 2012 Pew survey. Among eighteen- to twenty-nine-year-olds, 32 percent claim no religious affiliation. Even if they do have some vague belief in God or Christianity, younger people might like the idea that the speakers at Charlotte ONE don't get into the nitty-gritty or discuss divisive political issues.

Drew Gregory sums up his generation's mentality: "There's something about all the churches coming together that just feels right. Like we are all part of the same general cause. We don't get caught up in the details that really take away from what we're striving to do, to really change people's lives." Gregory worries that "a lot of people can get caught up in the semantics about what the Bible says about this topic or that topic, but really that's not important. What's cool is that Charlotte ONE is something where they can all come together."

Gregory and others have noted to me that diversity is extremely important to this generation. The crowd at Charlotte ONE is overwhelmingly white, but there are some Asian, Hispanic, and black faces. Diversity, though, is about more than race. As Gregory says, "We're used to growing up with people of different backgrounds and all denominations. It's not like we're part of some exclusive club." And so the people of Charlotte ONE like the idea that in this place Christians whose divides can seem unimportant can come together.

Whether Gregory's explanation will be heartening to most religious leaders, many of whom believe that the details of faith are important, is hard to say. And it remains a question whether devotion to the "general cause" is pressing enough to keep people in the fold. But even if some pastors are willing to make the tradeoff—Charlotte ONE may mean that young adults find our denominational differences less important, but they are more likely to come to church and we won't have to have a special young adult ministry—is Charlotte ONE a positive development on the whole?

One question about these collaborative efforts is whether they serve the larger cause of religion in public life as much as they serve individual churches. Rodney Stark, codirector of the Institute for the Study of Religion at Baylor University, is a skeptic who argues that competition among churches—including "aggressive marketing" of the wow factor kind—has helped to boost church membership. "It sounds good to save money and have one big deal instead of lots of smaller programs," he tells me. "But who is going to do the work? What really builds church participation is congregations getting their members to bring their friends and neighbors to church."

Stark says he has moved around a fair bit during his lifetime. And he can tell right away which churches in a particular area are growing. "If the folks from that church have knocked on my door or sent me a card. It's called working." When he was living in Seattle a few years ago, for example, he says, he attended a church that was so popular their "first Sunday service was Saturday night." The Bible camp offered horseback riding, karate, and Spanish classes. "Every kid wanted to go to their Bible camp."

Stark recalls that when he took some European friends to the church, "They cringed." "It's so unseemly," they told him. Stark's response? "So are empty churches." In fact, his point is that Europe does not have the kind of church competition that the United States has. There is no attractional church. In fact, few people are attracted to church at all. For many centuries, of course, it was simply a state-run church, and then religion slowly started to fizzle entirely. While reported weekly church attendance in the United States has hovered at around 40 percent for the past few decades, regular church attendance in European countries has plummeted. In 2007 the BBC reported that only about one in ten Brits attend weekly. Even among the more traditional Catholic countries, signs of life in the pews are few. Only 20 percent of Spaniards attend weekly, according to the 2004 European Social Survey.

Stark argues that competition has made America a more vibrant religious marketplace. In recent years the same argument has been made about South America and Africa. As missionaries fight to gain converts in the southern hemisphere, more and more people are becoming religious.

But Europe's religious climate is a legacy of state-run churches. When for centuries the government mandates church attendance and adherence to religious law, a certain spiritual element of the faith is lost. Too, the faithful begin to associate church with corrupt government bureaucracies rather than humble Christians seeking salvation.

The problem in Europe was not too much church collaboration, so it is hard to imagine that widespread cooperation among religious institutions in the United States will result in the kind of moribund religious environment that Europe has experienced.

Moreover, competition has real downsides, and not just financial ones. The leaders of the Charlotte ONE collaboration call the competition approach "sheep stealing," as in poaching from the flock of other churches, and they say that it isn't very Christlike behavior. Over time, religious leaders can begin to focus on aspects of a church that have little to do with spiritual life—karate, horseback riding, and so on—to the detriment of serving the spiritual needs of its members. The attractional church can cease to be much of a church at all.

Is there reason to worry about so-called consumer Christianity? Don't we simply live in a consumerist society and churches are like our other institutions? Perhaps. But seeing a company go under because another one made a better widget is not the same as watching a church have to close its doors because the one down the street has hipper music or a better social scene.

Even from a nonreligious perspective, competition has a cost. We don't want churches to pop up and go out of business after a few years. Long-term commitment to a church creates the kind of civic capital that every generation—even the millennial-born hipsters—could use.

Conclusion

"ALL YOUNG PEOPLE, newly come into an urban environment, and living for the first time outside of the family group and the association of old acquaintances, constitute an element of gravest spiritual and moral danger as well as one of untold possibilities." That's what University of Chicago sociologist H. Paul Douglass wrote in his 1924 volume, *The St. Louis Church Survey*. Douglass's response called for all hands on deck: "It is urged that all religious forces keep steadily in sympathetic touch with all these groups and that agencies particularly designed to serve them receive increased united support."

The problem of young, unattached adults wandering away from the religious reservation is hardly unique to our era. And while our current time seems to have brought with it a variety of different challenges in this regard, it has not brought too many new solutions.

Perhaps the most striking element that is absent from the accounts of successful religious institutions in the preceding chapters is technology. When I asked the academics, religious leaders, and journalists who cover religion which institutions were doing the best job and how, my respondents barely mentioned Facebook, Twitter, Pinterest, or Tumblr, let alone the institutional websites that congregations often spend thousands of dollars and hundreds of hours creating.

The young adults I interviewed seemed to expect a basic level of technological literacy from their churches and synagogues. According to a Pew study, 75 percent of millennials have a profile on a social networking site, compared with only 50 percent of

Gen Xers and 30 percent of boomers. Of course, they would like to see an updated Facebook page from their religious institutions with information about where services will be or what time events will take place, but I could not find one example of a technological innovation that brought someone into one of these religious institutions or an instance in which it convinced them to stay.

As for the millennial who told journalist Hannah Seligson, "What people in the past may have gotten from church, I get from the Internet and Facebook. That is our religion"? Well, count me skeptical that this attitude is widespread. Even David Kinnaman, who argues that technology has changed young adults' attitudes toward institutions—making them more likely to sample religious content from a number of different sources rather than committing to one—does not suggest that emerging adults actually see Facebook as providing the community or the spiritual content they would find in a church.

The effects of technology on young people's lives have been corrosive in many cases. One young woman sums up the situation to the author Samantha Henig in her book *Twenty Something*. The woman describes being out with a small group of friends for an evening event at a museum with food and beer and music. "My friend Annie pulled out her BlackBerry and began reading something: 'I'm reading an email that doesn't matter,' she said, sort of instantly baffled. 'I don't know why I'm reading this email.' I didn't, either. But I've been there."

Young people still want to have friends and a community and evenings at museums with beer and food and music. In fact, much of social networking is actually employed as a means to meet up with others. The Internet is not a substitute for community or religion. And all the time that young people spend in the virtual world may make them appreciate community all the more when they are with real live people. Of course, they still may compulsively check their smartphones and they may worry that they should really be somewhere else, but when they find a community they want to be a part of, they will participate.

This community need not simply be a roving urban tribe, as Kinnaman and others have described it. As Pastor Ray Cannata has shown through his work with Redeemer Church in New Orleans, young people want something very traditional: geographically based community, otherwise known as a neighborhood.

We needn't go too far down the road of psychoanalysis to speculate why. Many young adults were raised by parents who didn't let them go down the street by themselves, and those children now come to adulthood realize that they missed out on something. They watched plenty of *Sesame Street* growing up, but the idea that kids would be outside in the park, on the stoop, or playing in the street without constant adult supervision and an arranged playdate must have seemed completely foreign. Lenore Skenazy, author of *Free-Range Kids*, writes that parents for the past couple of decades have had access to twenty-four-hour news coverage of abductions and all sorts of other horrifying things happening to children. These cases don't happen now any more than they used to, but as Skenazy notes, "We're swimming in fear soup—fear of lawsuits, fear of injury, fear of abductions, fear of blame."

Today, twenty- and thirty-somethings, single or married, are desperate for the kind of freedom and spontaneity that living in a real neighborhood imply. When they go looking for an apartment to rent or buy, they tell their agents they want to be able to walk to everything. It's not just that they want to use less gas to help the environment (and their wallets) or they want the convenience of having a grocery store down the block. It's that they like the idea of running into people they know—at the coffee shop or the bar or even at a church. Though they might have only watched it in reruns, they want to live in a neighborhood that resembles a giant Cheers, where everybody knows your name.

It seems counterintuitive that people who are at a stage in their lives when they *can* be completely mobile—not tied down by a career or family—actually want to feel the sense of long-term belonging that a real neighborhood offers. Indeed, Robert Wuthnow, author of *After the Boomers*, tells me that when "people are in their twenties and don't have kids, there is no reason why they should be interested in their neighborhood." He says that neighborhood doesn't matter until they have kids and the kids are "getting ready to go to kindergarten."

Maybe it shouldn't matter to them, but increasingly it does. These people know it may be many years before they marry and have kids. But they still want to live in a place where they can be part of a community, even if they don't ultimately settle there for the long term. As we saw from Charlotte ONE, a religious institution can be part of the reason that young adults do decide to put down roots.

Many millennials experience this sense of neighborhood for the first time at a residential college. Eating meals together, living near each other, and running into each other at various places on campus seems artificial to many. College students inevitably describe their campuses as "bubbles." But truth be told, they like the bubble—not necessarily because it protects them from all sorts of realities they'd rather not deal with (getting a job, cooking and cleaning for themselves, knowing of the terrible things going on in the rest of the world), although it does that, too. What appeals particularly about life at a residential college is the sense of belonging.

When it comes to religious life on campus, this point is doubly true. Where colleges were once a primary force undermining religious belief among young people, now the young people who are not college educated are the ones who are less likely to be religious. Indeed, student religious life is flourishing thanks to the growth of campus Christian organizations, Muslim Student Associations, and Hillel.

Religious leaders off-campus suggest that they have a tough time getting young people to attend regular services in multigenerational settings after college because people that age have become used to "gourmet liturgy" or "Christian raves," as one pastor called some evangelical worship events. I'm not sure it's actually the content of church that seems like a letdown, though that may be part of the problem. More so than missing the large bands or the intellectual excitement of being in a campus religious group, young adults miss the community. When they graduate, young adults have to start from scratch to become a part of such a community. In college, they prayed and volunteered and studied religious texts with their friends—people their own age, with whom it was easy to relate.

After college, it is harder. People arrive at churches from all different places in life, and re-creating that sense of camaraderie that religious practice in college brought with it can be hard. And no one likes to go alone. This issue came up again and again in my interviews. Young people were nervous about trying out a new religious service on their own. What if they didn't know the hymns? What if no one spoke to them? If they could find just one friend to go with, they told me, it would have been so much easier.

One of the most interesting parts of the Alliance for Catholic Education (ACE) is the idea that the teachers fresh out of college live in community with each other, that they will experience that period of life with others in the same boat. The four or five teachers in a community will find a parish and a service they like together. They will start to incorporate pieces of Catholic life in their home together. The administrators who run the program will not, for the most part, tell the teachers how to live. But participants will be encouraged to live a more Catholic life when they are surrounded by their Cathlic peers.

Similarly, the young women I met living in a Moishe House in New York described how they didn't focus much on living Jewishly after they finished college. But when they were offered the chance not only to share an apartment with other Jewish women but also to host events centered on the Jewish holidays and lead service projects with a Jewish focus, the three of them jumped at the chance. Sure it's subsidized housing in Manhattan, but the three had found what so many millennials are looking for: a community with a sense of purpose.

The teachers in ACE and the young professionals who live in

Moishe Houses are living in more than just a postcollege dorm. They agree to take on a leadership role—to represent religious ideas to others and to welcome strangers into their circle. The people in charge of these programs are asking young men and women to "own the faith." Though they are not missionaries in the traditional sense, these kinds of programs—with their longer-term commitments and their structure of putting young adults on the front lines, so to speak—seem to have a deep impact.

The fact that years (even decades) after their participation in the program ACE teachers continue to attend alumni events—and not just happy hours, but weekend-long religious retreats and monthly Mass—suggests they have been affected. Many of the people who chose ACE did so because they wanted to do some kind of service.

According to the Pew Millennial Survey from 2010, people from this generation ranked "helping others in need" above owning a home, living a very religious life, and having a high-paying career. The only things ranked higher were being a good parent and having a successful marriage.

The evidence on whether they actually live out these values, though, is mixed. A 2012 study published in the *Journal of Personality and Social Psychology* found that millennials were actually less politically and civically engaged than other generations. They were more likely to volunteer, but the study was based on surveys of high school seniors and college freshmen, so it probably reflects a lot of school-mandated volunteering (an oxymoron, of course), rather than young people helping out on their own initiative.

But some evidence shows that service has a certain kind of cachet for this generation. An acceptance letter from Teach for America is harder to come by these days than one from a top law school. In 2010, 18 percent of Yale University's graduating class applied. And there is evidence that service—serious, long-term sacrifice requiring service—is one way for religious communities to attract young people. The religious content may even be secondary to start. They want to join a church-sponsored Habitat for Humanity program or volunteer to make sandwiches for the poor at their mosque. If they hear religious messages while they are there, well, so be it.

For some of the men and women I interviewed, there seems to be a connection between the importance they placed on neighborhood and the importance they placed on service. They like the idea of helping out in their own communities rather than traveling across town. This approach seems to necessitate urban living, at the very least. It's hard to reside in a leafy suburb and at the same time serve your needy neighbors.

Obviously, ACE offers its participants this kind of urban experience. Serving at an urban Catholic school and living nearby doesn't appeal to everyone, but many of the graduates seem to want to relive the experience after the program is over, moving into economically mixed neighborhoods.

A number of the ACE teachers told me they were not entirely sure about the religious aspect of the program initially. But by the time they were done, Father DelFra's characterization of the ACE teachers as a kind of lay order was not far from the truth. And just like members of religious orders, these young people are entering local parishes—many of which do not have a reputation for being particularly friendly to twenty- and thirty-somethings— and changing them. In other words, they are founding, or at least jump-starting, their own postcollege religious communities.

The Mormon mission, which usually lasts eighteen months, is the most intense version of this rite of passage for young adults. Not only do participants agree to devote a long period of time to this pursuit, but they are almost completely cut off from their friends, family, and popular culture. Missionaries have limited access to phones and are only allowed to communicate with their families once a week by email.

This experience doubtlessly has the effect of helping young Mormons to own their faith; knocking on doors and pitching your religious beliefs to strangers definitely seems to make young LDS men and women stronger in their beliefs. But it also raises the question of how to be reintegrated into the regular religious community. For many returning missionaries this is not a problem, but for some, going from a life in which spreading the gospel is the most urgent and only task you are asked to do every day to a life in which your church really only needs you a few hours a week is difficult.

The Young Single Adult wards (YSAs) are tasked with ensuring that young Mormons, whatever their previous experience, feel like they are vital to the community's success. A community in which all the leadership positions, with the exception of one, are held by men and women under the age of thirty seemed at first foreign—even funny—to its members. But over time they have grown used to it and come to truly appreciate the experience and friendship with a common purpose that such structure has brought them. The bishop in American Fork is often faced with twenty-somethings who are still playing video games in their spare time. But he says to them: You are ready for real responsibility. He asks them to handle the community's finances, to teach theology to younger members, to reach out to people who are in need.

But if you do not have a separate community for young adults, how do you make sure that young adults actually get the leadership roles they need to feel needed? Keeping young adults in the congregation means managing the expectations of the older generation as well. Pastor DeForest Soaries jokes about firing his wife from her role in the church. But he is right that if older adults feel territorial about their positions, younger adults will stay away. And as churches now regularly include members living healthy, active lives well into their eighties, the twenty- and thirty-somethings could have a long wait before they naturally inherit any of those positions.

In many ways, it is very practical for religious leaders to ask these younger adults to start shouldering more responsibility. If people in their later thirties and forties are at the height of their careers and are needing to devote their time to childrearing, then younger adults are the people who really can afford to give more hours to supporting religious institutions.

Similarly, the bishop in lower Manhattan tells the somewhat older members of his YSA community that he realizes they are adults the rest of the week. They have high-paying jobs where people invest a lot of responsibility in them. He knows that they are capable of handling the work of running a religious community. And while he understands there are distractions of all sorts in New York, he expects them to take their faith as seriously (if not more so) than their careers. Though many of them are far from home and family, they should not forget about their obligations to find spouses and eventually have children of their own.

When it comes to speaking of marriage, religious leaders must negotiate a delicate balance. The majority of the ones interviewed in this book suggested that they don't spend a lot of their sermons talking about the need for their congregants to pair off. Having a specific ministry for singles in a traditional church is simply not appealing to most of them, and the young adults seem to appreciate that they are not pressured. But religious leaders don't mind acting as the occasional nudge. For the bishop in American Fork, that means talking to young adults about dating with a view to marriage.

Few of the young adults I interviewed actually met their spouses at a religious institution. In fact, many of them told me that dating people inside the congregation can be a little awkward. What happens if things don't work out? You'll have to see this person all the time. One change in behavior that many religious leaders have noticed is that maintaining friendships and continuing to be comfortable in a community is sometimes more of a priority than finding a romantic partner.

The Birthright Israel experience seems to be an exception. Having participants meet a spouse is one of the stated goals of Birthright funders. And even those who don't meet a spouse on the trip extend their social circles when they return and date friends of Birthright friends.

Even if they don't meet their mate directly through these experiences, though, religious institutions can still have a significant effect on the way people date and marry. As Ray Cannata, pastor of Redeemer in New Orleans, told me, "You find somebody, you're dating them, you realize that you can marry them, [then] don't wait. Go ahead." He tells his congregants, "People need to get married younger. Part of the reason why divorce rates are high is people marry too late. They have too much baggage. By the time they finally get married, they've been practicing singlehood for too long and they don't know how to shift gears. They also have so much in their background, they've dated so many other people and have had so many other serious relationships and learned that they can break it off, they take that attitude into their marriage."

Most of the religious leaders I interviewed agreed with this sentiment. They want to ensure that singles don't feel uncomfortable or out of place in the church, which can certainly happen, but they also want to encourage couples who have been dating for a few months (and certainly a few years) to take the next step. The danger, as these religious leaders see it, is couples who continue to date indefinitely, worshipping the "God of other options."

———

For young adults who are not willing to commit to a two-year teaching stint or an eighteen-month mission or three years of living in a Moishe House together, shorter experiences like Birthright or short-term mission trips can get young adults excited about a faith community.

But the trick, more and more religious leaders are coming to realize, is that in order to harness the kind of energy that those experiences create, there needs to be some kind of pipeline connecting them to a more permanent institution when they return. The Birthright trips that happen for college students seem to have less of a lasting effect than those that are for people in their early twenties which draw from people all living in one community. When a bunch of twenty-somethings living in the Washington, DC, area return from a Birthright experience, they are immediately invited to participate in other Jewish gatherings—even gatherings that happen inside of synagogues. They can continue to socialize with people from their trip indefinitely since they all live close together.

The idea of setting foot inside a religious institution can be very intimidating to young people, as we have noted. For young Muslims, going into a mosque carries all sorts of connotations with which they may not be comfortable. For them, a mosque represents an older generation stuck with an immigrant mentality. They worry about listening to sermons with an occasionally bigoted and often homophobic view of the world. They do not understand much of what is said during religious services because they are in another language. To make it all more difficult, they worry, particularly in the wake of 9/11, about how non-Muslims see them.

Again and again, the young adults I interviewed told me that finding a diverse community was of great importance to them, which is not surprising. According to Pew, millennials are more racially tolerant than any generation before them. For instance, Pew reports, "Compared with older groups, particularly Americans ages 50 or older, Millennials are significantly more likely to be accepting of interracial marriage. While 85 percent of Millennials say they would be fine with a marriage to someone from any of the groups asked about, that number drops to about three-quarters (73 percent) among 30- to 49-year-olds, 55 percent among 50- to 64-year-olds, and just 38 percent of those ages 65 and older."

Even within their religious communities, young Muslims

would like to see people of different races and ethnicities. (This was certainly true of the Christians I interviewed as well.)

For mosques that are interested in this generation, a sensible approach is to first find a way to gather young men and women inside of each other's homes or in restaurants or parks so that they can find a sense of community; then find the institution after that. Programs like Theology on Tap, in which lectures on religious topics are offered in bars or restaurants, were first sponsored by Catholic dioceses. Now the format has been adopted by a variety of Protestant churches as well.

While the setting is less intimidating, at some point, religious leaders need young people to make that leap. Maybe they will meet other people at Theology on Tap or at the MECA gathering who will make them feel like it's okay to come to a real worship service. And the fact that leaders from MECA are starting to take positions of leadership at the Islamic Center of Southern California (which sponsors MECA) suggests that a pipeline is being built. These younger leaders will force their mosques to become less ethnically homogenous, more multilingual, and more open to the younger generation.

Meanwhile, MECA is working to build up that sense of community. It wants to grow a critical mass of twenty- and thirty-somethings who will volunteer to do some kind of service work or who will simply go on hikes or play tennis together. Particularly for religious minorities, this sense that "There are others out there like you" can be an important draw. But even for Christians, a regular church can sometimes seem socially limiting, even though many of the young adults I interviewed suggested that they enjoyed having older mentors in a congregation.

Indeed, this generation has much less of a rebellious streak than previous ones. According to the Pew report on millennials, this generation has had fewer spats with their parents than their parents had with their own parents. While difficult economic times may have forced many of this generation to "boomerang" back to living with their parents, these adult children have not complained too much. As Katherine Newman wrote in her recent book *The Accordion Family*, "What is different now is that the intimate lives of the coresident generations, the boomers and their kids, are carrying on under the same roof." She attributes this change to "a desire to support and admire the new person this adult child has become."

Whatever the reason, more than six in ten millennials, according to Pew, "say that families have a responsibility to have an elderly parent come live with them if that parent wants to." Compare that number to fewer than four in ten adults age sixty and older who believe this. All in all, there is no reason to think that young adults are so averse to including older adults (or for that matter, children) in their communities.

Young people are "conflicted" on this point, says Christian Smith of Notre Dame. "They like the homogeneity of being with people like them, but they intuitively sense that to be part of something bigger is a good thing." Smith finds that the "churches that are most successful are those that combine both. They have a full age range of people in a well-rounded community, but they also invest in young adult ministry and/or get a critical mass of young adults showing up."

Plenty of churches, however, simply can't get that critical mass because of too much competition or not enough of a population. In Charlotte, it seemed that the problem was the former. Charlotte ONE has allowed young people to have it both ways—to be part of something bigger, an intergenerational church, while getting to be with their generational peers once a week. Though the leaders at Charlotte ONE are concerned that they are on occasion providing too much of that campus ministry experience—the Christian rave that has created the problems for them in the first place—they also believe that they have found a way to transition young people into that multigenerational, traditional church experience.

In some ways those in the millennial generation really might be different from their parents and grandparents. In a 2012 article called "The Cheapest Generation," *Atlantic* editors Derek Thompson and Jordan Weissman speculate on the ways that the Great Recession has permanently changed the spending habits of millennials. The biggest change, they argue, is that these young men and women don't want to purchase the two most significant expenditures that young adults make—houses and cars.

Many of us can hardly understand how it's possible to achieve independence from one's parents, let alone become a real grown-up, without these things. But these young adults simply don't have the money—or the jobs to make the money—that they need.

The religious institutions that are successful realize that this generation doesn't have much to contribute financially. Many of them are not in the habit of giving even a small amount. But what if churches, instead of being yet another line item in the budgets of millennials, actually helped them to think about being good stewards of their money? The approach of First Baptist of Lincoln Gardens is drawing in young adults who haven't given a lot of thought to financial matters and helping them get off on the right foot. While they are considering how to rid themselves of debt, many consider the importance of tithing as well.

The young people who attend Bible study each week at Lincoln Gardens have rejected the prosperity gospel model—in which faith is merely a vehicle for getting rich—not only because they believe its theology is inauthentic. They are also turned off by the showiness of its leaders. They complain of the hypocrisy of pastors who preach that they are concerned for the poor but spend thousands of dollars on expensive suits and cars and jewelry. Something about the slickness of these leaders gets under the skin of the young adults I interviewed.

Hypocrisy is one of the worst sins for this generation, and it is one reason that some scholars say young adults stray from religion in the first place. Kara Powell, a professor at Fuller Theological Seminary, tells me that her research on teenagers has found that they tend to think of faith as "external." Powell, the author of *Sticky Faith: Everyday Ideas to Build Lasting Faith in Your Kids*, tells me that young people have a "Jesus jacket." She says, "They graduate from college and toss the jacket into the corner" because they want to experiment and do things that are not in keeping with their religious traditions. But here is the key: "Even if they want to pick it up they don't know how. They feel guilty, they feel full of shame." They don't want to put on the jacket unless they are living a fully Christian life. This is, needless to say, a high bar, and it presents religious leaders with serious challenges. How do you convince young adults that they can put the jacket back on . . . or that faith is not really a jacket at all but something much more ingrained?

The religious institutions described in this book appeal in part to this generation because they feel authentic. The people, the programs, even the buildings where they are housed do not feel slick. They do not feel like the results of consultants meeting with focus groups. Some of the leaders of these institutions, like Charlotte One and Birthright NEXT, have thought specifically about how to get twenty-somethings reengaged. But others have a mission in mind that is broad and urgent, and if it appeals to millennials, well, all the better.

In a 2013 article in *Leadership Journal* titled, "Why I Won't Give to Your Church: An Honest Letter from a Millennial Believer," Robert Jewe tried to explain his generation: "We've been 'marketed to' since childhood, and we can smell it a mile away. When we step into a church and sense it, it's patronizing and offensive. Your 'Young Adult Outreach' may be well intentioned, but it comes off as phony."

Religious leaders who are successfully connecting with young adults realize that sleek advertising is not going to bring people into the pews. The barriers to entry are not matters for a public relations firm to tackle. Young adults want community. They want a neighborhood. They want a critical mass of people their age. But they want to see older people and younger people in their religious institutions, too. They want a way to serve, and many of them want a way to serve sacrificially for longer periods of time. They want the racial and ethnic diversity of the country reflected in their religious community. They want a message (in English) that resonates and helps them tackle the practical challenges they face, of which there are many. They want to feel welcome whether they are single or married. And while they may appear to be experiencing an extended adolescence, when they are given responsibility, they are often inclined to take it.

Notes

1. Before we go too far down this road, let's define "young adult." The millennial generation includes those born after 1980. I think it's fair to include people between the ages of eighteen and thirty-four when discussing young adults. There is a tendency among some communities to include people later in their thirties and even their forties as young adults. But as a recent article in the *Jewish Week* notes, President Obama would have been a "young adult" when he was first elected to the Senate, Martin Luther King Jr. would have been a young adult when he organized the Montgomery bus boycott, and Tony Blair would have been a young adult when he became prime minister of England. Extending "young adult" past a certain point becomes absurd.

2. See W. Bradford Wilcox, Andrew J. Cherlin, Jeremy E. Uecker, and Matthew Messel, "No Money, No Honey, No Church: The Deinstitutionalization of Religious Life among the White Working Class," in *Research in the Sociology of Work* (forthcoming).

3. When we talk about emerging adulthood, we are often talking about the middle and upper-middle classes in America, since these are the groups who generally have the luxury of putting off adult responsibilities. Most of the young people interviewed for this book have gone to college. Though only about 40 percent of the population had attained an associate or bachelor's degree as of 2012, the young people with college degrees are often the ones in the best positions to take responsibility for the leadership of religious institutions. There are, however, some new groups, like Launch, a ministry specifically devoted to non-college-bound young adults to help them discover and maintain religious connections.

4. Riley, Naomi Shaefer. 2013. *Til Faith Do Us Part: How Interfaith Marriage is Transforming America*. Bethesda, MD: Oxford University Press.

5. Riley, Naomi Shaefer. 2013. *Til Faith Do Us Part: How Interfaith Marriage is Transforming America*. Bethesda, MD: Oxford University Press.

Index

Note: page numbers followed by
"n" refer to endnotes.

The Accordion Family (Newman),
151
Adas Israel, Washington, D.C.,
85–87
adolescence, extended, viii, 91–92
Advocates for Catholic Schools,
60–63, 68–69
Adzima, Megan, 58–60, 62
After the Boomers (Wuthnow),
141–142
age
faith, correlation with, 4
integration vs. segregation by,
12, 26–27, 36, 102–104
of leadership, transition in,
107–110
Alliance for Catholic Education
(ACE), 57–63, 66–72, 143–144,
145
Arabic language, 40
assimilation and Muslims, 48–49
atheism, 7, 9, 110–111
attendance, religious. *See also*
religious nonparticipation or
noncommitment; *specific cases*
older people, overrepresentation
of, 4
passing of expectation of, 6, 9,
110–111
steady, long-term decline in, 8

attractional church, 134, 137, 138
authenticity, 30, 152, 153
authoritarianism in black
churches, 112

Barna Group, 3, 5, 127
Barno, Whitney, 113, 116–117
Berger, Peter, 5
Bergler, Thomas, 12, 114
Bible and theology of place, 22
Birthright Israel program, 73–77,
148, 149
Birthright NEXT, 77–83
black churches
authoritarianism in, 112
civil rights movement and, 110,
115
class and, 111, 120–121
drift away from, 110–111
economic messages and
prosperity gospel in, 116–121
First Baptist Church of Lincoln
Gardens, Somerset, NJ, 107–
109, 112–121
inner cities vs. suburbs and, 111
leadership age transition in,
107–110
preaching and, 112–114
relevance vs. traditionalism in,
113–116
social gospel and, 120
Blalock, Ryan, 126, 133–134
"boomerang" generation, 151

Boston Advocates for Catholic
Schools, 60–63, 68–69
Boyle, Tatiana, 94, 96
Bronfman, Charles, 73
Brooks, David, 13–14
Bryfman, David, 83–84

campus ministries
churches hurt by, 11–12
church membership and, 26–27
Muslim Student Association
(MSA), 43, 50–51
"wow factor" and, 124
Cannata, Ray, 19–25, 27, 30–31, 34,
141, 148
career as distraction, 99–100
Carey, Jessica, 32–34
Carmel Baptist, Charlotte, NC,
128–129, 134
Carmichael, Stokely, 115
Catholic Church
Advocates for Catholic Schools,
60–63, 68–69
Alliance for Catholic Education
(ACE), 57–63, 66–72, 143–144,
145
church teachings, dissatisfaction
with, 65–66
Hispanic immigrants and ethnic
shift in, 111
Jesuit Volunteer Corps and
Urban Catholic Teachers, 58,
71–72
in New Orleans, 22–23
Nuns on the Bus, 65
parishes, theology of place, and,
22–23, 63–64
priests, nuns, and brothers, drop
in numbers of, 55
service ethic and social justice
tradition in, 56, 58, 66
strategic decisions faced by, 64

women, role of, 64–66
Cattan, Shukry, 46, 50–51
Charlotte ONE (Charlotte, NC)
Charlotte urban context and,
129–131
collaborative nature of, 123, 128,
135–138
connecting to local churches,
131–135
evangelical/mainline
cooperation and, 126–128
launch and goals of, 123–125,
128–129
sermon messages of, 125–127
wow factor and, 124, 134–135
Chaves, Mark, 4, 8, 11, 15
"The Cheapest Generation"
(Thompson and Weissman),
151
children, 10, 49–50, 92. See also
family and parenting
choices and options, 1-3, 132
churchgoing. See attendance,
religious
Church of Jesus Christ of Latter-
day Saints. See Mormons and
the Church of Jesus Christ of
Latter-day Saints (LDS)
church shopping, 63–64, 101, 127–
128. See also Shabbat Hopping
cities and urban areas. See also
place, theology of
Charlotte urban context, 129–131
churches and urban roots, 18–19
Mormons in New York City,
99–101
New Orleans, 25–26, 28–29,
31–32
return of people to, 17–18
City Center (Keller), 18
class
black churches and, 111, 120–121

emerging adulthood and, 155n3
Mormon marriage divide by,
    97–98
religious affiliation and, 5–6
cohabiting, 10
collaboration among churches,
    123, 128, 135–138. *See also* Char-
    lotte ONE (Charlotte, NC)
college-educated young people,
    focus on, 15, 155n3
college students
    belonging, community, and,
        142–143
    campus ministries for, 11–12,
        26–27, 124
    Muslim Student Association
        and, 43, 50–51
    reasons for not going to church,
        26
Comisar, Emily, 79
community. *See also* place,
    theology of
    ACE and, 57–58, 143–144
    church consumers and, 20
    church presence in, 23–25
    individualism vs., 21
    MECA and, 150
    Moishe Houses, 81–82, 143–144
    need for, 29–30
    neighborhood sense, connection
        to, 23, 141–142, 145
    residential colleges and, 142–143
    service, connection to, 145
community service
    Catholic Church and, 56, 58, 66
    Judaism and, 85
    millennials and importance of,
        144–145
    Muslims and, 38, 52
    "servant leadership," 60–61
competition among churches,
    136–138

"The Consequences of Free"
    (Bryfman), 83–84
consumer mentality, 20, 69, 138
Cooper, Barry, 2–3
Corpening, Charles, 115–116
costs of joining a Synagogue,
    84–85. *See also* finances
Crouch, Andy, 19
cultural traditions and Muslims,
    41–45

dating, 1, 96–97, 100, 134. *See also*
    marriage and intermarriage
*The Death and Life of American
    Cities* (Jacobs), 22
DelFra, Fr. Lou, 57, 60, 63, 68–69,
    71–72, 145
D-Free (Soaries), 116
diversity
    Charlotte ONE and, 136
    ethnic shifts, 111
    importance placed on, 44, 48,
        149–150
    theology of place and, 31–32
Douglass, H. Paul, 139
Duckworth, Bishop Cory, 91–92,
    95, 97, 98, 102–103
Duckworth, Cameron, 91, 98

Eastern Orthodox Churches, 44
economic downturn, effect of, 10
economic messages, 116–119
Ehrenhalt, Alan, 17–18
"emerging adulthood." *See also*
    millennial generation
    class and, 155n3
    moral reasoning, lack of, 7–8
    as second or extended
        adolescence, viii, 91–92
    technology and, 8–9
    worries about, 3
ethnic diversity. *See* diversity

Europe, 137–138
evangelical Christians, 47, 126–129
evangelization, 12, 19. *See also*
    missions experiences

Facebook, 33, 89, 139–140
family and parenting. *See also*
    marriage and intermarriage
    fear among parents, 141
    helicopter parents, 13, 91–92
    millennials' relationship with
        family, 150–151
    Mormons and, 92
    nonparticipation and family
        patterns, 10
Fennell, Liz, 69–71
Fennell, Mark, 62–63, 71
finances
    Black Church messages on,
        116–119
    Judaism and, 83–85
    prosperity gospel, 119–121, 152
    spending habits and resources
        of millennials, 151
First Baptist Church Nashville,
    114–115
First Baptist Church of Lincoln
    Gardens, Somerset, NJ, 107–
    109, 112–121
Fort, Nyle, 120
free programs, issue of, 83–85
Free-Range Kids (Skenazy), 141

Garner, Marty, 24, 29–30
Garner, Rachell, 23
Garson, Jenna, 74
geography. *See* place, theology of
Gerrol, Rachel, 87–89
Gibson, Shane, 31, 32–33
Girl Meets God (Winner), 102
God Is Alive and Well
    (Newport), 4

Good Shepherd United Methodist
    Church, Charlotte, NC, 128
Gottschalk, Russell, 78–79
Graham, Billy, 12
*The Great Inversion and the
    Future of the American City*
    (Ehrenhalt), 17–18
Gregory, Drew, 130, 135–136
growth efforts and programming,
    21
Grumley, Rachel, 63–64

Hamid, Jahan, 51–52
Hancock, Jay, 128–129
Hashem, Mazen, 41, 51
Hebrew language, 40
helicopter parenting, 13, 91–92
Henig, Robin Marantz, 2
Henig, Samantha, 2, 140
Herberg, Will, 44
Hickman, David, 123–124, 126–127,
    129–130
Hodes, Rachel, 81
home groups, 30–31, 79–83
homosexuality, attitudes toward,
    47
hopping. *See* "shopping" for
    congregations
Hussein-Cattan, Meymuna, 39, 45
Hymowitz, Kay, 97–98
hypocrisy, 119–120, 151–152

immigrants, 41–42, 111
individualism, 13–14, 21
infantilization or juvenalization of
    young adults, 12–13, 91–92
institutions, distrust of, 7, 13–14
intermarriage. *See* marriage and
    intermarriage
Internet and technology, 1, 8–9,
    139–140
Islam. *See* Muslims and Islam

Islamic Center of Southern California, 35–36, 38, 43, 49, 52, 150. *See also* MECA

Jackson, Jesse, Jr., 118
Jacobs, Jane, 22
James, Lisa, 108–109, 113–114, 117
Jefferson, Anthony, 119
Jesuit Volunteer Corps, 58, 71–72
Jethani, Skye, 133
Jewe, Robert, 153
Jews and Judaism
    Birthright NEXT, 77–83
    free programs vs. membership costs and, 83–85
    Hebrew language and, 40
    marriage and, 76–77, 89
    Moishe Houses, 81–82, 143–144
    people vs. culture vs. religion, 76
    Shabbat Hopping, 85–89
    Taligt-Birthright Israel program, 73–77, 148, 149
    welcoming, issue of, 86–87
Johnson, Jason, 103–104
Jones, Taylor, 95, 102
Justice, Leigh, 131–132
The Juvenilization of American Christianity (Bergler), 12, 114

Kalish, Maxie, 81–82
Keller, Timothy, 18–19
Kelly, Rob, 134
King, Martin Luther, Jr., 108, 120, 155n1
Kinnaman, David, 8–9, 11, 140, 141

Lagerman, Jenna, 131
language, 40, 44
LDS. *See* Mormons and the Church of Jesus Christ of Latter-day Saints
leadership responsibilities for

young adults, 36, 95–96, 144, 146–147
Levin, Morlie, 77–78, 79, 80–81
Lewis, John, 115
Lowy, Jenna, 86

mainline/evangelical cooperation, 126–129
Manchester, David, 76–77
Manning, Pat, 67–68
Manuela, Roshell, 104
marketing to young people, 12, 136, 153
marriage and intermarriage
    interracial marriage, Millennials and acceptance of, 149
    involvement efforts aside from marriage, 105
    Jews and, 76–77, 89, 148, 149
    Mormons and, 91–93, 96–98, 100, 104–105
    Muslims and, 48, 50
    religious institutions and, 147–148
Marsh, Ashley, 24–25
McDaniels, Eric, 110, 111–112, 119
McKenna, Eileen, 23
MECA (Muslims Establishing Communities in America), Santa Barbara, 35–41, 48–52, 150
megachurches, 13, 19, 109, 133
millennial generation. *See also* "emerging adulthood"; *specific cases*
    as "boomerang" generation, 151
    choice paradox, decision paralysis, and, 2–3, 132
    consumer mentality and, 20
    individualism and institutional distrust in, 13–14
    religious nonaffiliation among, 6

millennial generation. (*continued*)
traditional aspects of religion
among, 7
Miller, Rabbi Aaron, 87
Miller, Stacy, 87
Mission Adulthood (Seligson), 89
missions experiences
ACE and, 57–58
Birthright Israel, 73–77
Christian short-term missions,
75–76
Mormon missions and
returning Mormon
missionaries, 95, 145–146
mobility and migration, 34, 82.
See also immigrants
Moishe Houses, 81–82, 143–144
Moore, Russell, 9
moral reasoning, 7–8
Mormons and the Church of Jesus
Christ of Latter-day Saints
(LDS)
children and families and, 92
leadership responsibilities and,
95–96, 146–147
marriage and, 91–93, 96–98, 100,
104–105
in New York City, 99–101
returning missionaries and
transition issues, 95, 145–146
Young Single Adult wards
(YSAs), 93–97, 100–104,
146–147
Murray, Charles, 5–6, 97–98
music, 27, 64, 86, 114, 124
Muslims and Islam
Arabic language and, 40
college students and, 50–51
community service and, 38, 52
cultural and religious identity,
tensions between, 41–45

homosexuality and other
religions or cultures, attitudes
toward, 47–48
immigrants and assimilation
issues in America, 41–42,
48–52
MECA, Santa Barbara, 35–41,
48–52, 150
religious education and studying
Islam, 39–40, 46–47
women, attitudes toward,
45–46
Muslims Establishing
Communities in America
(MECA), Santa Barbara,
35–41, 48–52, 150
Muslim Student Association
(MSA), 43, 50–51
Myers Park United Methodist
Church, Charlotte, NC, 126

neighborhood, sense of, 22–25,
141–142. *See also* place,
theology of
Newman, Katherine, 151
New Orleans, 25–26, 28–29, 31–32
Newport, Frank, 4
New York City, Mormons in,
99–101
Notre Dame University, 56–57, 59,
60, 63
Not Without My Daughter (film),
43
Now, Elder Steven E., 94
Nuns on the Bus, 65

older adults, overrepresentation
of, 4
options and choices, 1-3, 132
Otten, Becky, 25–26, 28, 29
Owens, Latasha, 117

parents. *See* family and parenting
Paulson, Jessica, 94–95, 96, 102
Peacock, Richard, 111
Pecheny, Yelena, 130–131
Pew Forum on Religious Life, 3,
    6, 48, 127
place, theology of
    Bible and, 22
    black churches and, 111
    Catholic Church and, 22–23,
        63–64
    diversity and, 31–32
    mobility, challenge of, 34
    neighborhood sense and, 22–25,
        141–142
    urban life and, 17–19
Polonsky, David, 86
Porter, Becky, 86
Powell, Kara, 152
preaching and sermons
    in black churches, 112–114, 119
    Charlotte ONE and, 125–127
    hypocrisy in, 152
    Muslim Khutbahs, 50
    at Redeemer Presbyterian, New
        Orleans, 22, 24
Pride, Nicole, 108, 117
prisoners, 52
programs, emphasis on, 20, 21
prosperity gospel, 119–121, 152
Protestant, Catholic, Jew
    (Herberg), 44
Protestant denominational lines,
    127–128

racial diversity. *See* diversity
Redeemer Presbyterian Church,
    New Orleans
    Cannata's background and
        philosophy, 19–21
    college students and, 26–28

mobility as challenge for, 34
New Orleans, social action, and,
    25–26, 28–29
theology of place and, 22–25,
    31–34
Reeves, Ashley, 103
Reidhead, Melissa, 100–101
relevance
    black churches and, 113–116
    Charlotte ONE and, 125
    Islam and, 38, 46–47, 50
    Jewish collectivity and, 81
Relief Society (LDS), 94–95
Religion among the Millennials
    (Pew Forum), 6
religious nonparticipation or
    noncommitment. *See also*
    specific cases
    reasons for, 8–13
    secularization trend, 4–6
    stigma, fading of, 6, 9
    young adults and, 3–4
responsibility-taking and leader-
    ship roles for young adults, 36,
    95–96, 144, 146–147

Sabbath and Mormons, 100
Saunders, Brenda, 99
Saxe, Leonard, 74
Schmitt, Mandy, 126, 127
secularization trend, 4–6
Seligson, Hannah, 89, 140
Semel, Beth, 87
sermons. *See* preaching and
    sermons
service. *See* community service;
    social justice
Shabbat dinners, 79–83
Shabbat Hopping, 85–89
Shapiro, Mark, 74
shared reality, lack of, 8

Shifa, Homaira, 39–40, 41
"shopping" for congregations.
    See also Charlotte ONE
    (Charlotte, NC)
  church shopping, 63–64, 101,
    127–128
  Shabbat Hopping, 85–89
Sixth and I synagogue,
    Washington, D.C., 87
Skenazy, Lenore, 141
Slater, Dan, 1
Smith, Brian, 75
Smith, Christian, 7–8, 9, 10–11, 151
Smith, James Michael, 124, 125–
    126, 128
Smith, Kelly Miller, 114–115
Smolen, Shoshana, 81, 83
Soaries, DeForest, 107–108, 112–
    113, 116–121, 146
Soaries, Donna, 107–108
social gospel, 120
social justice, 29, 56, 64
social networking, 33, 89, 139–140
Souls in Transition (Smith), 7–8
Sparks, Evan, 76
Stark, Rodney, 4–5, 136–137
St. Bridget's Catholic Church,
    Boston, 62–63, 70
Steinhardt, Michael, 73, 76, 77
Sticky Faith (Powell), 153
The St. Louis Church Survey
    (Douglass), 139
Synagogue membership costs,
    84–85. *See also* Jews and
    Judaism

Tabor, Will, 23, 26
Taligt-Birthright Israel program,
    73–77, 148, 149
Teach for America, 28, 56–57, 144
technology and Internet, 1, 8–9,
    139–140

text interpretation and Muslims,
    39–40
theology. *See also* place, theology
    of
  in black churches, 115
  church collaboration and, 127
  extra-institutional, 7
  prosperity gospel, 119–121, 152
  traditionalist theology, rejection
    of, 11
Theology on Tap, 150
Thomas, Arthur, 112–113, 116
Thompson, Derek, 151
Thompson, Kim, 29
"Timothy generation," 110
The Triumph of Christianity
    (Stark), 4–5
Turk, Jihad, 35, 36–38, 43, 48–50
Twentysomething (Henig and
    Henig), 2, 140

Urban Catholic Teachers, 58

Ver Beek, Kurt, 76

Warren, Rick, 109–110
Washington Hebrew
    Congregation, 87
Weiss, Aimee, 82–83
Weissman, Jordan, 151
welcoming, issue of
  age segregation question and, 36
  black churches, relevance, and,
    114, 121
  Judaism and, 86–87
  MECA and, 38, 51
  mosques and, 46
  neighborliness and, 31
Wells, Bishop Mark, 99–100, 104
Wermly, Chris, 97, 101–102
"Why I Won't Give to Your
    Church" (Jewe), 153